£1-

TOWARDS A ROYAL COLLEGE OF TEACHING

Raising the status of the profession

Contents

Editor's foreword

Charlotte Leslie MP
Member of the Education Select Committee

In a lesser known work, *Choruses from the Rock*, the poet TS Eliot writes of the folly of 'dreaming of systems so perfect, that nobody will need to be good'. It is sage advice for politicians.

When patients get superb care from the NHS, it is not from a system but from a dedicated professional going the extra mile. Great education is also thanks to the dedication, expertise and professionalism of the people who teach. Systems have their place but the values, vocation and expertise of those who work in those systems are what creates success – in other words, somebody needs to be 'good'.

Indeed, the success of our nation depends on its people and our nation's future success depends on the next generation of our workforce and our next generation of parents. And who has one of the largest parts to play in the development of these future generations? Our teachers.

But, despite the vital importance of teaching, teachers do not enjoy the same status as other professions. Why?

This booklet not only looks at why teaching lags behind in professional status but also puts forward a powerful solution: a Royal College of Teaching.

Royal colleges and other professional bodies have promoted and protected the status of professions like medicine for, in some cases, hundreds of years. And the more you look at issues like the encroachment of the state into the classroom, the lack of a clear practice-based career progression for teachers, or the linking of academic education studies and evidence with the realities of the classroom, the more a 'royal college' shaped hole seems to emerge.

This hole has become so evident that the Education Select Committee, on which I sit, has recommended that the teaching profession look to establish a Royal College of Teaching. The Select Committee is not alone; the Academies Commission recently came to the same conclusion. An idea that has been hanging in the air until now has perhaps found its time.

There is a caveat. In its response to the Select Committee's report, the government supported the idea of "'a member-driven independent professional body" which could certainly… enhance the prestige of the profession.' It rightly stated: 'to be successful, the impetus for such a body must come from the profession itself.'

This is absolutely crucial. A Royal College of Teaching cannot be another government creation. It cannot come from a politician like me but must come from teachers themselves.

So, this booklet begins to demonstrate the ever-growing support from teachers and educationalists from across the educational landscape for the idea of a Royal College of Teaching and for reclaiming the professionalism of teaching.

The contributors do not put forward a strict prototype for a College or specify exact details of what it should look like. Importantly, this is not written by politicians (you'll probably be relieved to know that this is the last you'll hear from a politician in these pages). It is an exploration of the challenges and opportunities setting up a Royal College of Teaching could present.

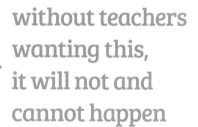

without teachers wanting this, it will not and cannot happen

It includes contributions from beyond the world of education, with insights from a long-established medical college – the Royal College of Surgeons – and the recently founded College of Emergency Medicine. It also contains a case study of professional status in engineering – a different, though similarly diverse, profession.

Crucially, it includes contributions from those working in education from across the spectrum: trade unions, primary school teachers, subject associations, teaching leaders, those involved in continuing professional development, and many more. It looks at the various functions a Royal College of Teaching could usefully perform, and is a starting point to find out what teachers themselves would want from it — if, indeed, teachers want it at all.

Because without teachers wanting this, it will not and cannot happen.

I would also like to thank several key individuals, without whom this booklet would not have been published. The wisdom and expertise of Professor Chris Husbands, Director of the Institute of Education, have been invaluable, as have that of Professor Derek Bell and Dr Raphael Wilkins of the existing College of Teachers, David Weston of the Teacher Development Trust and, of course, the contributors themselves.

The generosity of our sponsors, AQA, and the guidance and hospitality of the Royal College of Surgeons have been fundamental to this exploratory first step towards a Royal College of Teaching. I would also like to thank the Prince's Teaching Institute, which is contributing so much to the exploration of the reality of a Royal College of Teaching.

Now it is over to teachers, and anyone who wants to see teaching gain the professional status it deserves, to make this happen. Read, agree, disagree, set out your thoughts. Please engage and give us your feedback. This matters. If we get this right, we will be transforming the status of perhaps the most important profession of all for good.

Supporting great teaching

Andrew Hall
Chief Executive, AQA

Teaching deserves higher recognition. Teachers are at the heart of the education system, making a difference every day to the lives of hundreds of thousands of young people.

When I have travelled to or worked in other countries and spent time with teachers, I have seen how much time is devoted to their development and the currency they have within society. Great teachers in this country deserve the same recognition.

That is why AQA is supporting the publication of this series of articles, written by a wide range of contributors, who want to promote the debate around the concept of a Royal College of Teaching.

Royal colleges exist for a number of professions, nineteen in all, and provide a single expert voice for those who work in areas like medicine. They provide a structure where issues of mutual concern and interest can be shared and debated.

As an education charity that works with and supports thousands of schools through our qualifications and continuous professional development courses, AQA wants to join with others in exploring how a new organisation could promote the expertise and professionalism of teachers.

The proponents of this idea are not suggesting that a Royal College of Teaching would replace the important role of trade unions. Indeed, a

teaching
deserves higher
recognition

number of them have written for this booklet. It would promote the quality of teaching but would not stray into the area of representing union members' interests.

At a time when our school system structures have changed radically, with many different types of schools, a single body could bring teachers together and play a critical part in enhancing public perceptions about the profession.

A royal college could gain greater attention for the rich body of research evidence that exists in education, designed to help teachers, and which my own organisation contributes to through its Centre for Education Research and Policy (CERP).

This debate is a real opportunity for teachers to get involved and share their views on how a royal college might work so that their collective professionalism is recognised.

A Royal College of Teaching could provide a much-needed boost to the status of the teaching profession and ensure that we have a guardian for teaching standards that maintains confidence in the quality of teaching.

Introduction: the importance of professionalism

John 'Louis' Armstrong CBE
Chairman, Professions for Good

If there had been an Olympic gold medal in London for professional bodies, Team GB would have won convincingly.

Admired across the world, British professionals and their professional institutions have a long and proud history. There are now over 200, many governed by Royal Charter. In the Middle Ages only three classical professions were recognised – divinity, law and medicine. Later, there were debates about whether two more should be added – armed service, and education.

But the concept of a professional goes back much further. The ancient Greeks understood what it really meant. To be a true professional, Plato argued, required not only mastery of knowledge and practical skills but also, critically, being disciplined in moral excellence. By adopting this concept over 2,000 years later, those who founded the modern professional bodies struck gold.

It was all about the insistence that professional and technical expertise was only a part of the equation. What mattered as much, or even more, were values, attitude and behaviour, and an altruistic approach, with the clients' needs firmly to the fore.

The Victorians knew what had to be done to build a modern, thriving economy in a globalising world, and to construct a progressively more educated and sophisticated society. The mid-19th century saw the flowering of professional institutions, whose modernised versions still play invaluable roles today. Engineers, solicitors, architects, surveyors and accountants, for example, are all professionals whose institutions date from that era. Standards were set, examinations introduced, rules of conduct enforced, and status raised.

But without teachers – arguably the most important profession of them all – no one would have become sufficiently educated to go on to gain a professional qualification of any kind.

So, in this great blossoming of professionalism and respected institutions in almost every other sector over the past 150 years, why have teachers somehow missed the boat?

Not all teachers will fit neatly into a box labelled 'the teaching profession' or, indeed, want to. Some may believe the profession is better off as it is. But surely they deserve to have the opportunity to qualify as members of a single prestigious governing body for their profession? They merit both the status and the reputation for professional excellence and integrity implicit in their meeting and maintaining their institution's high standards.

Why has it not happened? There are many possible reasons. Among them, perhaps, is the historic association of education, the church and the profession of divinity. Monks and clergymen dominated the ranks of intellectuals and academics from the very earliest times. My own school, King's Canterbury, was a foundation of St Augustine in 597, and headmasters were always canons of Canterbury cathedral. Many older universities began life with the prime purpose of educating clergy. Even in the 16th century, schoolmasters had to be licensed by the church just to teach grammar.

what could be more important for our country's future?

There were no craft guilds set up around the medieval teaching world. Many of these guilds in other sectors morphed into the origins of modern professions, despite having some characteristics of trade associations. Perhaps the special status accorded to teachers in society throughout history, and their 'quality assurance' by the church, meant that teachers didn't see a need, even by the 19th century, to coalesce into a recognised profession, and form a national professional institution.

What a shame! The beauty of an independent professional body, working in the public interest as prescribed by Royal Charter, is that it can combine setting professional standards, awarding qualifications, creating and enforcing a rigorous code of conduct and set of values, having an effective regulatory framework, providing thought leadership, formulating research and policy, and sharing international best practice. While not perfect, many other countries are keen to emulate this 'royal college model'. Why not one for teaching in this country?

There are wide-spread advantages to society in less visible ways, too: the feelings of self-respect, status, pride and, most importantly, of obligation that come with belonging to a high calibre, independent professional body.

Without that, the teaching profession has suffered. My sister taught in the same state school for nearly forty years. Through her I have been aware of some of the damage done to generations of children (not to mention their teachers!) by successive political agendas: changing ideologies, passing fads, lack of evidence-based policies, teachers feeling ignored and under-valued, endless bureaucratic impositions and constraints – the list is long and well documented, with collateral damage to teachers' morale and effectiveness very apparent.

There are many exciting initiatives now underway in the field of education, including the revitalisation of the profession. A royal college could be the glue that binds all these together.

As chairman of a collaborative group of professional bodies formed to promote the virtues and value of the professions as a whole, I look forward excitedly to the day when we are joined by a Royal College of Teaching. It would demonstrate how much we value our most critical profession. What could be more important for our country's future?

A medical royal college perspective

Jonathan Shepherd CBE FMedSci FRCS
Professor of Oral and Maxillofacial Surgery,
Cardiff University

Summary

In the context of the development of a Royal College of Teaching, this article describes one of the largest professional membership organisations in medicine, The Royal College of Surgeons of England (RCS). The reasons for its foundation and its structures and functions are summarised, together with its role and culture as the professional home and national voice of surgery and surgeons. With no trade union or health service management roles, and entirely funded by surgeons themselves with the express purpose of advancing surgical standards and patient care, the RCS is independent, authoritative, innovative and standard-setting. Career advancement to substantive UK hospital posts is only possible through the demonstration in RCS membership and fellowship examinations of competence in surgical science and the practice of surgery. The RCS provides UK surgery with a rudder through constantly changing political and managerial cross currents, a long-respected advisory role for government, and, most importantly perhaps, a headquarters for surgery from and through which the natural instinct for improvement, which characterises every profession, can be capitalised on to raise standards. This article also explores the extent to which these functions could usefully be applied to a Royal College of Teaching and the limits of a medical analogy.

The history of the Royal College of Surgeons

The creation of the RCS by Royal Charter in 1800, when the standing of surgery and surgeons was low and reforms of the existing Company of Surgeons' by-laws were urgently needed, was motivated by the ambition to increase the status of what was a trade guild founded in the 14th century to an institution worthy of a profession and to provide a base for academic study. A home was also needed for an extensive collection of anatomical and surgical specimens, which continues to be the basis of the museums at the RCS.

Faculties and resident specialist societies

The RCS is the professional home of surgeons of all surgical specialties. It hosts the offices of the societies of the ten recognised surgical specialties.

The faculties of dental surgery (dental specialists) and general dental practice (family dentists) are the national home of the dental profession.

The evolution of professional bodies in medicine has resulted in the development of nineteen medical royal colleges, some of which, like the Royal College of Obstetricians and Gynaecologists, the Royal College of Anaesthetists and the College of Emergency Medicine (A&E specialists) developed from the Royal College of Surgeons. This diversification reflects the individual strong identities, experience, bodies of knowledge and skills that define the major branches of medicine. This evolution has also led to a forum for the medical royal colleges where issues of mutual interest and concern are debated.

Basic role and remit

The Royal College of Surgeons of England is an independent professional body and registered charity committed to setting, promoting and advancing the highest standards of surgical care. It has education and training, research support, assessment and examination, advisory and policy roles. It also has wide international influence and a portfolio of highly valued medals, awards, lectures and other incentives to excel.

Education, training and examinations

The RCS provides postgraduate education categorised as core (education relevant across all surgery) and specialist (relevant to particular recognised specialist surgery such as neurosurgery and orthopaedics). Education and training are delivered in blended distance-learning programmes supplemented by a variety of short courses at the RCS to support surgical trainees who, like all trainees except those taking time out in full-time research (see below), are all practising in hospitals full or part time. These programmes are flexibly structured so that learning can be tailored to match particular training posts and are designed according to UK surgical curriculums developed by the RCS with partners from government and the other surgical royal colleges to help prepare trainees for RCS membership (MRCS) and fellowship (FRCS) examinations. Success in these examinations is evidence of the acquisition of knowledge and competence to specified

pre-eminent among the advantages of the College are political independence, lack of any trade union interests, ownership by its members, and sharp and constantly adjusted focus on advancing standards

standards at core and specialist levels respectively and is essential for career advancement to NHS specialist training and consultant posts. The RCS awards various other diplomas which, on their own, are not sufficient for RCS membership or fellowship.

Education materials include clinical case summaries with discussion, banks of multiple choice questions and answers, study modules and reference materials relevant to the various sections of RCS's examinations. As part of these programmes, the RCS also supports communities of trainees at various levels, providing opportunities for peer discussions, subscription to a journal popular with trainees, ('I read it on the tube, bus or between patients. The figures are really good – you can absorb a lot of information in a short amount of time'), discounts on RCS examination preparation courses and access to other learning resources. The RCS also delivers workshops designed to introduce medical students to surgical practice.

RCS Education develops and delivers short courses, none more than three days duration, and programmes across all the surgical specialties and sub-specialties. Specialty portfolios are managed by teams of tutors who work with their specialist associations. Courses, delivered in the RCS's high tech skills labs, build on the foundations of core training and cover the operative procedures and anatomical knowledge essential to trainees in each specialty. The RCS provides masterclasses across the surgical specialties, bringing renowned surgeons to debate topical subjects and share knowledge and skills.

Multiprofessional (eg, teams from the armed forces) and continuing professional development courses are also provided in areas such as legal aspects of surgical practice, patient safety in theatre and training and assessment in practice.

The RCS is a partner in formal arrangements to enrol trainees in surgery and dentistry. Committees comprising government, and doctors and dentists from medical royal colleges and universities, assess evidence of training completion, following which, if this evidence is available, the RCS issues the certificates which are essential for advancement to an NHS consultant post. The RCS takes a strong interest in developing academic surgeons – the professors of surgery of the future. Dedicated training programmes have been developed for them that integrate surgical training with research.

Advisory roles

As a national professional body made up of practising surgeons across the UK and more widely, the RCS sustains a wide range of formal and informal relationships with university medical and dental schools, NHS postgraduate education (organised in NHS deaneries), practice regulators (General Medical and Dental Councils), NHS services and clinicians' trades unions.

Capitalising on its specialist knowledge across the whole of surgery, the RCS provides government with detailed workforce data and needs-forecasts and recommendations on training priorities.

The RCS has a range of advisory roles that include, at a national level, formal board membership of NHS bodies responsible for ensuring that education, training, and workforce development drives the highest quality care and that investments in education and training are transparent, fair and good value for money.

A network of RCS advisors in surgery and dentistry provide advice in every health region in England and Wales and in every specialty. These advisors scrutinise and approve consultant surgeon job descriptions and are statutory members of selection panels on which NHS trusts and health boards' depend for appointments to consultant posts. Advisors also take part in annual assessments of trainees to help assure a suitable mix of clinical cases across training schemes, all of which involve trainees rotating through several hospitals.

Research support

The RCS funds around twenty-five new one- or two-year full-time research scholarships in surgery and dentistry annually, which comprise full clinical salary and consumable costs and are based in university teaching hospitals. Reflecting that academics in surgery all practise surgery as well as teach and lead surgical research, the RCS promotes clinical research, integrates the production of evidence of effectiveness (often derived from clinical trials) with training and practice, and provides research mentorship.

practice in both professions is
a craft, an art and a science,
carried out according to a
defined ethical framework

The RCS also manages its own research grant competitions, which are supported by the proceeds of investments and ongoing fundraising. Its academic and research board brings together university surgeons from across the UK to maintain the productive and strong links between research, training and practice, which are at the heart of advancing surgical standards.

International role

Reflecting its long history and links, particularly with Commonwealth countries, many of which host RCS courses and examinations, the RCS identity and brand is well recognised in surgery internationally and the RCS provides advice and lecturers in many countries. Diplomates' ceremonies, where distinguished surgeons from around the world are honoured as well as those who have passed RCS examinations, have a strong international flavour and are often attended by two or even three generations of fellows and members from the same family.

Policy development

The RCS provides independent advice for government and NHS trusts, and information for patients and the public. It publishes position statements, surgery statistics and standards for surgical practice. It responds to government and other consultation requests and holds policy seminars on key issues in surgery.

Prizes, awards and incentives

The RCS awards prizes, lectureships and medals, which are highly sought after by their recipients and revered throughout surgery. The Honorary Gold Medal instituted in 1802, for example, is awarded 'for liberal acts or distinguished labours, researches and discoveries eminently conducive to the improvement of natural knowledge and of the healing art', and the Lister Oration is supported by the 1920 Memorial Fund in memory of the pioneering surgeon, Joseph Lister.

According to rigorous selection standards, the RCS makes recommendations and contributes citations for its fellows and members in respect of national honours and clinical excellence pay awards. Together with its portfolio of prizes, this support provides a range of powerful incentives to excel in surgery and to contribute to the RCS's work.

Functions the College does not have

The RCS has no interest in terms and conditions of employment, negligence insurance, practice (as opposed to training) regulation, NHS management, acting as an association of hospitals, or educating medical and dental undergraduates. While Lord Nuffield founded RCS chairs in both surgery and anaesthetics, these research posts have long since been devolved to university medical and dental schools.

Advantages of the Royal College of Surgeons

Pre-eminent among the advantages are political independence, lack of any trade union interests, ownership by its members, almost all of whom are practising surgeons working full time in the NHS, and a sharp and constantly adjusting focus on advancing surgical standards. Its value to its members is best illustrated by the membership attrition rate being close to zero, despite an annual membership fee representing about 0.3% of salary after tax. The respect in which it has been held by governments of all political complexions, and continues to be held by the current coalition, is clear. Its longevity reflects its success in evolving, continuously, its education programmes and examinations to reflect and assess the best in surgery and dentistry, and in maintaining a set of incentives to excel.

The RCS's journals, comprising the heavyweight, scientific *Annals*, two dental journals and a widely read news *Bulletin*, which includes regular state of the nation statements by the President, helps ensure that, based on reliable evidence, the RCS leads and promotes constructive change. A further safeguard against resistance to progress is the regular election, by RCS fellows spanning the profession, of professors of surgery (who lead surgery research) and surgeons who are NHS clinical directors (who lead services in their hospitals) to the RCS council and board of trustees.

Most importantly perhaps, the RCS provides UK surgery and surgeons with a rudder through constantly changing political and managerial cross-currents, and a national home from and through which the natural instinct for improvement, which characterises every profession, can be capitalised on to raise service standards.

Barriers and limits

As well as limiting its own functions as described, the RCS is limited by the extent of its influence. While this influence is substantial and has remained so with regard to its core functions, influence can and has changed at the margins depending on the extent to which government and universities involve themselves with professional practice. Its power to implement policy in hospital practice is limited. Compared to teaching and policing, for example, the RCS has little interest in management and leadership training. The provision of leadership training, mainly through the National College of School Leadership, is a strength in education from which the Royal College of Surgeons may usefully learn The surgical royal colleges in Edinburgh and Glasgow limit the influence of the RCS in Scotland.

Challenges faced by the College

The relationship between the RCS and national UK government is synergistic and when either neglects its core functions and its check and balance role, things go wrong; maintaining this relationship and relationships with other bodies is a constant challenge. It helps that surgery is a mature profession but change and evolution is continuous at one interface or another.

The body of knowledge that defines surgery grows continuously and not just with regard to effective new medical tests and techniques; many practices once seen as beyond criticism, like hospitalisation for minor surgery and the prophylactic removal of wisdom teeth, have been found wanting. Measured and timely RCS leadership based on this constantly evolving evidence is a challenge that is recognised and met in the ways described above.

The RCS is one of nineteen medical royal colleges, which means that while it can be the voice of surgery and dentistry, it cannot be a voice or professional home for all branches of medicine. Liaison with fiercely independent surgical royal colleges in Scotland and Ireland is a challenge.

Continuous updating of training resources, quality assurance of assessment, responding constructively to government proposals, developing policy in the light of new evidence, and commentary for the media, are important and continuous tasks.

The limits of the medical analogy

Surgery and teaching have much in common, including a long history and tradition. They are practised predominantly in public-funded hospitals and schools and in comparatively much smaller private sectors. Teachers and surgeons are graduates with postgraduate training and qualifications, and work in and lead teams comprising professionals and support staff. Both professions include many distinct specialties, all of which have their own curricular and anatomical territory, societies, associations and support arrangements. Practice in both professions is a craft, an art and a science, carried out according to a defined ethical framework.

There are important differences, however. Undergraduate medical and dental courses are designed from the start to prepare students for professional practice and include education and training in clinical settings from an early stage – though to a lesser extent in the early years. After graduation, there are two years of managed foundation training carried out full time in hospitals or general practice. In teaching, arrangements are more diverse. The Teach First initiative, for example, is integrating teacher training with practice in schools likened to the 'teaching hospital' model in medicine, and government policy is, fitting with the medical training model, leaning in this more practice-based direction. In surgery, all academics practice whereas academics in teaching rarely practice in the school classroom. In surgery, from graduation, practitioners practise continuously and a 'Practice First' reform would not be necessary.

Healthcare professionals take a Hippocratic Oath prior to entry into professional practice but there is no equivalent in primary, secondary or tertiary education, or for headteachers. It has been observed by a national figure in education that, 'what it means to be a teacher is looser than ever'.

Given the numbers of school teachers, the scale of an all embracing Royal College of Teaching would need to be considerably larger than the Royal College of Surgeons which, in 2012, had a membership of 22,500.

What could a Royal College of Teaching take from the Royal College of Surgeons model?

This model of a professional body seems to have much to offer teaching and teachers. Most importantly, it offers a way in which the profession can establish, stabilise and sustain its national identity, values and high purpose, and lead the advancement of teaching standards.

It offers a transferable framework for setting national training standards though examinations and for the provision of education to prepare trainees for the success in these examinations, which is needed for specialisation and promotion.

The establishment of a college fellowship by examination – a high level teaching qualification that is essential for progression to the senior ranks of teaching – is attractive from a medical standpoint. Fellowship acquired in this way would also provide a single national electorate from which the college council, officers and trustees could be elected, including from the ranks of those employed by universities. A college membership examination could, applying this model, be developed to provide a national test and teaching qualification, including for those in training programmes like Teach First and undertaking education Masters degrees. This would be a solution to concerns about the variable quality of the many different routes into teaching. The college might develop a qualifying examination suitable for teachers from outside the European Union.

This model offers a self-funded advisory framework both nationally for government, and regionally and by specialty, comprising appointed advisors who would advise schools on appointments and job plans and sit on appointment committees. In time, the college would develop international standing and be a sought after source of advice on professional practice and training, and lecturers and examiners.

A Royal College of Teaching would, if this model is applied, have important roles in managing the transition of aspiring and trainee teachers from university to the classroom, and in ensuring that academic teachers continue to practise in schools – an important step for educational research and teacher training, and for children and parents. In surgery, full-time apprenticeship with practising trainers in the clinic (and the operating theatre after the end of foundation training – itself a full time apprenticeship across a wide range of specialties and general practice) is fundamental to learning the art, craft and science of surgical practice.

If this model is applied, a Royal College of Teaching would have important policy and communications roles independent, and seen to be independent, of any trade union role. This separation of functions would help both the college and the teachers' unions to discharge their responsibilities more effectively and transparently. The college would not carry out research itself but would, through scholarships, bursaries and grants, promote teaching research of direct relevance to the classroom, children and parents.

Every profession needs safeguards against resistance to constructive change and this model provides a transferable range of these, which include a portfolio of scientific and practice journals, integration of research, practice and training (reflected in surgery by the frequent election of professors and practitioner–directors to both the council and board of trustees), a set of powerful incentives to excel, and formal relationships with government and universities.

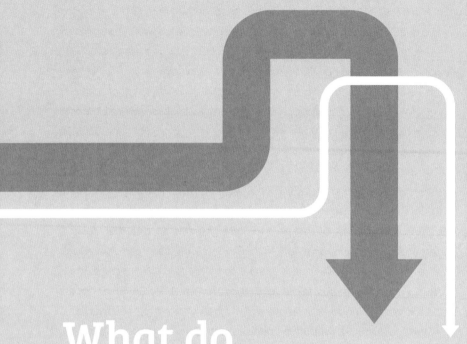

What do grassroots teachers need?

David Weston
Chief Executive, Teacher Development Trust

Teaching is one of the great altruistic professions. We join it to help others: to nurture their talents, to overcome the disadvantage of their backgrounds, and to share with them our joyful love of learning. Our work is a complex combination of art, craft and science that must be delivered instinctively and flexibly to large groups of children and young people with incredibly diverse needs, aspirations and enthusiasms. Our profession carries the hopes of society for the next generation, a heavy burden that we cannot possibly hope to deliver to everyone's liking and yet also an incredibly empowering and energising opportunity. It is time to create an organisation that will reflect our collective aspirations for the profession. It must represent our vocation and foster a sense of collegiality. It must inspire, support, and lead us to follow our passion and create ever better outcomes for children. It must discover the best of our practices and share them and then seek to do even better with innovative and rigorously evaluated research. Above all else it must recognise that we grow as teachers as we become more successful at helping our pupils and that the most skilled practitioners should be at the pinnacle of our profession. We will only stop politicians and the media lecturing us with their solutions to problems when we grasp the nettle and show that we can make the hard changes ourselves. Others will stop trying to force change on us when we are seen as trustworthy leaders of change.

We are, at present, a long way from this vision. There are very few ways to gain recognition of being an outstanding practitioner so our progression relies heavily on gaining administrative and management responsibilities. Our opportunities to learn are very limited, and much of the one-off lecture-style professional development that we undertake stands in stark contrast to the high quality interactive and experiential learning that we are now expected to deliver for our students. In many of our schools, 'research' has become a dirty word, a euphemism for yet another set of impractical ideas that have neither been explained nor suitably adapted to work in our classrooms.

The following three sections examine career progression, professional development, and use of research and evidence, in more detail, and are followed by some general recommendations.

Career progression

One of the first areas that a new professional body will have to get to grips with is the large structural change currently taking place in initial teacher education. There is a significant shift towards teaching schools being primary partners in relationships with higher education institutions as well as continued expansion of employment-based routes, including Teach First. A new body will need to take responsibility for quality assuring the multiple different routes and for sharing the most effective practices among teacher–educators.

In the final year of initial teacher education, applicants are assessed to see if they have reached the standards required for Qualified Teacher Status (QTS). These standards are maintained and updated by the government, with the most recent change being a simplification and streamlining that combined the qualifying standards with the core professional standards. Although there is a requirement to carry out a further year of teaching (the 'newly qualified teacher' or NQT year), there is a sense that once a teacher has QTS then they are 'fully formed' and ready to teach. Indeed, the government explicitly states that the same set of standards are expected to apply immediately post-qualification and thereafter, with headteachers required to use their own interpretation of expected progression.

This stands in contrast to many other nations (and professions) where the length of time required in an apprentice role is far longer and where further, higher standards (as judged by an independent body) are required in order to progress through the professional's career. In our current system there is no longer a requirement for a teacher to have QTS at all: headteachers may use their discretion to recruit anyone they wish. A new professional body needs to ensure that teachers' professional standards are suitably challenging and widely respected enough that they become effectively mandatory through the universal aspiration to achieve them.

There used to be options for specialisation via the Excellent Teacher (ET) or Advanced Skills Teacher (AST) statuses. These were paid positions that recognised outstanding teaching by external assessors. The AST position included a requirement to work with other schools. Even at their height, only around 1% of the teaching population went for these standards, although the government's target was to push on for 4%. However, both have now been withdrawn with a decision yet to be made about the requirements for the new Master Teacher standards which have been suggested as a replacement. The ET and AST standards were only available to teachers if a paid position was vacant, and this depended on the budget and school policy. The current suggestions around Master Teacher standards are that there will be no external assessment and that the position will be entirely at the discretion of the headteacher, guided by some standards created by the government. This means teachers' career progression relies on the willingness of their school to develop them.

There are a few semi-official professional standards, including Chartered Science Teacher, Chartered Geography Teacher and Chartered Assessor, which are organised by the relevant subject associations and bodies. However, there is no central coordination or oversight of these standards, they do not exist in most subjects and areas, and there is no clear progression beyond them. A new professional body needs to create a clear career structure with accredited paths for general practitioners, specialists (both subject and non-subject, eg behaviour or assessment) and leaders. Progression through these career paths must be achievable independently of schools' willingness or ability to promote.

Instead of pursuing specialism and higher professional qualifications, the majority of teachers take on extra responsibilities. Around four-in-five teachers beyond the fourth year of their career have taken on some form of responsibility for administration and/or leadership, whether that is as a coordinator (eg of a key stage within a subject), a head of year or department, or another leadership role. The eligibility for these roles is entirely in the judgement of headteachers – there is no defined standard that needs to be reached in order to progress.

The leadership pathway itself is not smooth. While a few ambitious teachers have reached headship in their early 30s, over 50% of current head teachers are in their 50s and planning to retire in a few years. Around one third of deputy headteachers have no plans to move in to headship, thereby acting as 'blockers' to those who wish to progress. Even so, nearly one-in-six primary teachers will become heads during their career (1-in-18 over the whole system) and this is significantly higher than other countries, which tend to have fewer larger schools (eg 1-in-54 teachers becomes a headteacher in Singapore). Once again, this highlights how the leadership pathway dominates in our system. While the leadership pathway should remain important, a new professional body must rebalance the career structure so that the majority of teachers are able to pursue general or specialist teacher pathways instead of having to gradually give up classroom practice.

Professional development

Unlike many other professions, there is no mandatory requirement to carry out a specific amount of professional development (aka continuing professional development, or CPD) as a teacher. The new teacher standards require teachers to 'take responsibility for improving teaching through appropriate professional development, responding to advice and feedback from colleagues'. The new performance management frameworks require schools to 'appraise teachers' development needs and help them identify any action taken to address [them]'. These are rather minimal and vague requirements that fail to adequately support the key principle that we only grow as teachers when we become more successful at helping our pupils.

The background research on CPD is rather stark. External courses are still the most common CPD activities for teachers to engage in and they are often preferred by teachers over other activities such as coaching, mentoring, peer collaboration and observation, academic study, etc. The reasons for this preference may be that courses can provide tips and tricks to solve problems, give breathing space from the day-to-day classroom work and help inspire new ideas. However, there is a wealth of solid research to show that courses by themselves are among the least effective ways of bringing about improved learning for pupils. The most effective ways involve working collaboratively through a process of sustained enquiry with an external expert to challenge and support.

In fact, not only is sustained, teacher-led CPD the most effective at improving exam grades for pupils, but also it leads to greater fluency and enjoyment of the subject among pupils, as well as increased motivation, confidence and enjoyment among the teachers. Mentoring and coaching have also been shown to be very effective ways to provide targeted assistance and challenge, especially when supporting new teachers.

The difficulty is that it is much easier, and generally more enjoyable, for teachers (or indeed anyone) to learn new ideas and try new approaches than to do the tougher work of examining, evaluating and painstakingly improving existing practices and habits. Every school year is filled with hundreds of new ideas, approaches and initiatives whether started by the teachers themselves or initiated by the school leadership team.

professional development should be tied explicitly to pupil learning rather than teacher practice

A new professional body will have a tough job to swing the balance away from the 'magpie-instinct' of always going for the shiny and new and to make the case that if we really want to help the children in our schools we must innovate with much more discipline – do less of it, sustain it, evaluate it, and ensure it impacts on our fundamental classroom outcomes. Progression through new professional career paths should be dependent on demonstrating this discipline.

The next important piece of work for the new body will be to ensure that the bulk of professional development is tied explicitly to pupil learning rather than teacher practice. At the moment a huge amount of CPD has aims like 'improve classroom management', 'teach the syllabus more effectively' or 'learn how to be a better head of year'. When CPD is chosen without first considering which pupils should benefit then there is much less likely to be any benefit to pupils at all. A lack of pupil learning focus makes it almost impossible to properly evaluate the impact of the training. In fact, research has suggested that only 7% of schools ever try and measure the impact of CPD on pupil learning – a shockingly low statistic. The new body must demand evidence that teachers have undertaken activities that have explicitly improved the quality of teaching and learning in their classrooms.

Part of the problem is the sense that responsibility for school improvement lies with the school leaders and not with the teachers themselves. CPD becomes merely functional: something that is 'done to' teachers to improve delivery and prepare talent for promotion. This is de-professionalising and disempowering. If we are to raise the status of the teaching profession then we must move to a culture where every teacher takes responsibility to improve outcomes for all children, not only within their schools and classrooms but also across the nation as a whole.

As the McKinsey Report[1] identifies so clearly, our best schools become self-improving because everyone takes collective responsibility for the maintenance and growth of their improvement. The best leadership of teaching and learning falls to all within the community.

Teams of teachers should be given the lead in school improvement projects where they identify learning that concerns them, research the most effective ways to improve it and then go through a collaborative process of improving their lessons and interventions to bring about the change. This process needs to be evaluated rigorously and then shared with the rest of their colleagues and the wider profession. CPD should become a collegiate effort at improving outcomes for children and young people and less about delivering pre-digested ideas to teachers. Our professional body must shy away from accrediting training hours put in and instead focus on rewarding and acknowledging successful practice that has demonstrably led to improved learning.

Research, evaluation and evidence

Through the work of leading academics such as John Hattie and Dylan Wiliam, we now know a great deal about the teaching practices that bring about the most effective learning. However, far too many teachers are unaware of the evidence of what works best and this has left the profession wide open to being sold snake oil. The fact that some teachers still argue that it's worth doing Brain Gym with their pupils, or that it is a positive benefit to label pupils as visual, auditory or kinaesthetic learning, should be a source of extreme embarrassment. A new professional body must find a way to disseminate best practices and quash misconceptions.

At the same time, the sharp separation of research and practice has left teachers isolated from the research evidence that could inform them. Education research is still mainly published in closed journals which are not available to teachers, and much of it is written in a way that is unhelpful for those trying to implement ideas. Whereas most medical researchers keep practising in hospitals in order to stay relevant and respected, the systems and structures in education and higher education make it almost impossible for the same to occur in schools. If teachers were given the opportunity to lead school improvement through collaborative enquiry and research then this chasm could be significantly narrowed, with researchers taking roles within the teacher teams and teachers being seconded for part of their time in to university departments. Our new professional body must work with schools and policy makers to remove the practical, financial and cultural barriers that prevent this from happening.

The teaching profession has had external accountability foisted on it and teachers' own judgements are almost invariably deemed as less important than those of external bodies or agents such as the exam boards and Ofsted. It is vital that we build a new capacity in the profession to construct assessments, design and carry out rigorous research-level evaluations, and produce reliable analysis of pupil progress in meaningful ways. We cannot, as a profession, complain that our judgements are not being taken seriously if we cannot back up these judgements with clear and scientific analysis. We cannot complain about the quality of evidence used to judge us if we do not produce better quality evidence ourselves. Our new professional body needs to raise every teacher's understanding of these issues. It must also ensure that every school has access to at least one expert who can help design assessments to tease out the subtleties of understanding and skill, produce rigorous quantitative and qualitative analysis of pupil progress and learning, and who can critically analyse the evidence behind research and suggested innovations.

Notes

1. Michaels E, Handfield-Jones H and Axelrod A. *The War for Talent*. Boston: Harvard Business Press; 2001.

A primary school perspective

Alison Peacock
Cambridge Primary Review Network Coordinator
and Headteacher, The Wroxham School

Primary and Early Years Foundation education is of fundamental importance. Writing as a primary headteacher and leader of a national network for the Cambridge Primary Review, I believe that the voice and influence of primary teachers and headteachers has become muted in recent years. There are many possible reasons for this but it is vitally important that this issue is addressed. This article sets out my rationale for the establishment of a Royal College of Teaching as a means to provide a principled, cohesive and authoritative professional voice about education in this country.

The final report of the Cambridge Primary Review recommended essential aims and principles for primary education. In my experience as a headteacher, conference speaker and network leader working with many primary colleagues, discussion and agreement about the core purposes of primary education is warmly welcomed, and can drive improvements in practice. Professional courage and strong leadership come from clarity of vision about what education should aim to achieve in the broadest sense. A Royal College of Teaching could help to establish the core purposes and aspirations of education for all children in this country.

The importance and necessity of high quality education should be universally understood and celebrated within our society. Professional status for the teaching profession cannot be demanded but will inevitably rise if unity and clarity of purpose are achieved. A teaching profession that is ambitious not only for schools but for the system as a whole, and that can demonstrate not only commitment but evidence of impact, will gain prestige.

Individual membership of the Royal College of Teaching would need to command wide-spread respect in order to draw colleagues from both maintained and independent schools of all phases and types nationally. Membership based on high quality experience and expertise would cut across the increasingly fragmented structure of schooling, to establish an irresistibly influential and informed body of colleagues.

There is a wide debate to be had about the structure, organisation and membership of a Royal College of Teaching, and it will be important that the structure of the College services the needs of children and young people rather than its own internal purposes. However, in order for the

College to achieve rapid and credible recognition at a system level, my own view is that membership at different tiers should be gained through a rigorous application process. Chartered membership of the College could be available to teachers after one year of teaching but only if they were able to evidence appropriate levels of experience, eg leadership of CPD, small-scale research, or contribution to the achievement of the school or department. Membership would require an annual fee from individuals and a reference from the headteacher. Beyond this, fellowship would be open for applicants with a minimum of five years of experience who could evidence further development within or beyond the school. Fellowship would also require an annual fee. Academic fellowship would provide a further tier that awards recognition for accredited further study at Masters or PhD level, where such study demonstrably contributes to improved outcomes for children. Although the College needs primarily to meet the needs of children and young people, our ambitions for them will be realised only if we can mobilise effort and support across the full range of education, so I would also suggest that honorary membership be awarded to academics and others working to further an ambitious, principled education system. Although there would be no fee for this tier of membership, there would be an expectation that such members would be willing to give their time to advisory groups and to support the overall quality of the organisation through contributions to research publications, attendance at conferences and so on.

Membership of the College would gain high status if it was attained through merit rather than through right. This would give the organisation a completely different ethos to that of the enforced membership of the General Teaching Council. It would not be a body for negotiation of teachers' pay and conditions. However, in exceptional circumstances it would exercise the right to terminate membership. The Royal College of Teaching would be characterised by the high calibre of members.

The rapid demise of local authority advice and support is particularly problematic for primary schools. In the absence of local authority guidance, a range of commercial organisations are selling advice to schools. There are 17,000 primary schools in England, many of which are at risk of becoming isolated and vulnerable. The proposed new structure of schools through academy chains has not been a solution for the vast majority of primary colleagues, with only 5% of primary schools moving to academy status. The Royal College of Teaching could provide all members with information and strategic advice and enable less confident leaders to feel supported through the knowledge that their role was aligned to principled, informed national leadership.

Local leadership of what David Hargreaves terms a 'self improving system' has led to a welcome flourishing of local and national networks. There are a range of organisations that primary colleagues can choose to align with, including, for example, federations and trusts, faith schools, teaching schools and alliances, academy groups, subject associations, local partnerships and trusts, unions and professional associations, higher education institutions (HEIs) and partnership schools, and major national organisations such as the Cambridge Primary Review and Whole Education. The importance of a Royal College of Teaching lies in the notion that such an organisation could form an over-arching network within which smaller networks would flourish independently. It could be that smaller networks would seek affiliation with the College in order to enhance their work.

In *Children, their World, their Education*[1], Robin Alexander called for a more research informed primary profession where: 'teachers should be able to give a coherent justification for their practices citing (i) evidence, (ii) pedagogical principle and (iii) educational aim, rather than offering the unsafe defence of compliance with what others expect. Anything less is educationally unsound.'

Perhaps the most important aspect of the future role that a Royal College of Teaching would perform would be that of raising the profile and prominence of educational research findings. The publication of the Sutton Trust Toolkit[2] with ranked, star-rated classroom interventions, has stimulated huge interest amongst primary colleagues. The Royal College of Teaching could learn from the impact that this presentation of evidence has had and could in future work in partnership with organisations such as the Education Endowment Fund to bring research evidence into staffroom and classroom discourse. A quarterly journal that provided the latest thinking and ideas alongside evidence of school impact would be very welcome.

In the last decade primary colleagues were inundated with 'best practice' models and toolkits via the Primary Strategy and its attendant field force of advisors. Much of the information sent to schools in the name of raising standards, was not referenced but was presented as a definitive model that only the bravest dare to challenge. However, there has been a backlash against this and there is now an increased appetite for policy that is informed by solid evidence rather than by political ideology.

It is most welcome that all teaching schools have to provide evidence of involvement with educational research prior to designation and are subsequently required to report on progress in this area among their alliance of schools. This drive to draw practice and research together is one of the most important features of the current education landscape. The concept of 'university training schools', although still at the planning stage, could provide a national platform to illustrate what can happen when pedagogy, curriculum and assessment practices are openly and actively informed by the latest educational evidence. The College would serve to disseminate new rigorous practice and to provide a counter to myths (such as the supposed impact of 'Brain Gym') that can become rapidly popularised in schools.

the answer is not to be found in reform of school structures but through the establishment of a national organisation with a collective purpose built on collaboration, professional integrity and the culture of ideas

The opportunity for College members to apply for small scale research funding would be hugely welcomed. Encouragement needs to be given to teachers to engage in further professional study and to publish their findings. A boost would be given to this expectation within teaching, if academic fellowship status could be gained within the College and if there was an expectation that publication of articles by classroom teachers and leaders was the norm, rather than the exception.

A *Lancet*-style journal from the College would publish findings from large-scale, funded projects and invite follow-on studies from members wishing to implement new practice within their school with the expectation that these would be peer reviewed and published. This would link the emerging work of teaching school alliances with that of HEIs, and individual study with the more traditional published educational research. Once more, the aim would be to provide a cohesive comprehensive message to the profession that would invite further exploration on an individual and school level leading to systemic impact.

There is an emerging role for CPD that is nationally accredited and quality assured. The new agency for school workforce reform, the National College for Teaching and Leadership, will offer a range of licensed courses. Other commercial providers and chains of schools are similarly engaged in the production of licensed training. The role of the Royal College of Teaching would be to offer CPD that was inspired by evidence and independent of political influence. Course providers and subject associations could seek quality assurance from the College in order that they could badge their CPD accordingly.

Annual membership of the College would entail recording CPD attended during the year. This requirement for an ongoing record of high quality professional learning would increase the demand for access to the latest thinking and would begin to lead the profession in a very positive direction.

Individual teachers join a union to provide them with collective bargaining power, protection, professional insurance, and the College would be no threat to the work and role of unions. Union membership would be wider than that of the College as all qualified teachers and trainees are eligible to join a union. The benefits to unions would be that the College would provide a single, united professional voice on behalf of chartered teachers which would be apolitical, informed by evidence rather than ideology, and focused on the pupil, not the practitioner.

Lobbying on behalf of the teaching profession has previously been largely in the domain of trade unions. The important role of the unions would remain but the College would seek to provide an apolitical stance that was a powerful guardian of quality, with a relentless focus on teaching excellence, not the teacher's interests. This would be a very welcome support for primary colleagues who may feel powerless to swim against the tide of the latest political whim. We need a national organisation to support schools against the current trend for initiatives linked to political imperatives, and we need to avoid the exhaustion that comes with feeling powerless to resist.

This government has demonstrated its power to achieve dramatic reorganisation of schools without legislation. Maybe we should learn from this and use it to our advantage. The answer is not to be found in reform of school structures but through the establishment of a national organisation with a collective purpose built on collaboration, professional integrity and the culture of ideas. The response from school leaders to accountability-led initiatives over the last two years has shown that when there is a perceived need for change in order to survive, radical reform can take place very swiftly. If collective courage could be built around an alternative model of school improvement associated with national recognition of core principles in education, maybe future governments would find it harder to exert undue influence than those of the past.

A culture of fear in schools is unhelpful and works against the aims of an accountability framework as it leads to inhibition and constrained curricular approaches. As a nationally recognised professional body of experts, the College could have influence on the appointment of Her Majesty's Chief Inspector (HMCI). An important culture shift would be achieved if HMCI (a supposedly non-political appointment) were to report regularly to the College as a means of ensuring quality and accountability.

This would shift the balance from an inspectorate that is inevitably influenced by political power to an inspectorate that is a guardian of quality informed by, and contributing to, the process of gathering evidence about pedagogy, curriculum and assessment that ensures education is fit for purpose.

This vision for a Royal College of Teaching that is ambitious for all children would represent the voice of English education across the world. It would be informed by and contribute to international evidence, and would engage in global debate. This knowledge base would provide a powerful counter to political temptation to 'cherry pick' and would encourage English educational policy to be inspired by rigorous comparative studies of international educational strategies and ideas.

Finally, but no less importantly, the College could have a transformative role in enhancing public perception of the teaching profession. Interestingly, the advertising campaign by the Teaching Agency, which sought to encourage new recruits to the profession, countered negative stereotypes that often typified the media's presentation of teachers and school leaders. We work with wonderful children and young people and yet positive perceptions of children are rare in our society. Once again, in raising the profile of the teaching profession, the College also has a role in providing real life, inspirational images and examples of the imagination and energy that children and young people bring to our society.

For the first time in English education, this initiative could have the potential to unite professionals regardless of the funding status of their schools, as they seek chartered status and recognition of their skills through membership of a prestigious royal college. The compelling vision of expert teachers and school leaders with an agreed ambition for education, would replace the existing fragmented school system in this country with a profession that embraces a collective responsibility for all children and young people.

Notes

1. Alexander R ed. *Children, their World, their Education: Final Report and Recommendations of the Cambridge Primary Review.* London: Routledge; 2009.
2. Toolkit. The Education Endowment Foundation. http://educationendowmentfoundation.org.uk/toolkit/ (accessed April 2013).

A secondary school perspective

Dame Joan McVittie DBE
Immediate Past President, ASCL
and Headteacher, Woodside High School

A Royal College of Teaching could – and should – fulfil several functions. Some of these are practical, but others represent ways in which such a college could re-position teaching as a profession with its own standards and responsibilities. First and foremost, a royal college should help to enhance the status of the teaching profession. Currently, when there are disciplinary or competence issues with *individual* teachers, it is all too easy for elements of the media to portray *all* teachers as being at fault. When the press are looking for comment from members of the teaching profession, they call upon the teaching trade unions, who often produce very polarised attitudes. Of course it is important that trade unions represent the interests of their members, but the voice of the profession is too easily lost in the views of individual unions. In contrast, when members of the medical or legal profession have behaved badly, somehow the press appear to isolate this individual from the other members of the profession. For example, the crimes of Harold Shipman did not by extension tar all GPs. If there was a royal college that could speak on behalf of teachers, and represent them in the media, then the perception of the public would be of a profession that was thoughtful, altruistic, committed and knowledgeable, nuanced and professional, as representatives of the Royal College of Teaching would present views that did not simply represent a sectional, union view.

In addition, having seen some of the effective models of royal colleges elsewhere, a key aspect would be the leadership of continuing professional development (CPD). This does not necessarily mean the *delivery* of CPD; it is important that schools and teachers are able to source this from a range of providers. However, it is equally important for the long-term quality of schooling that the delivery and quality of CPD providers' work is monitored. Currently, the National College for Teaching and Leadership (NCTL) is responsible for monitoring the quality of provision in leadership CPD for teachers, although it rarely delivers such CPD itself. However, with externally provided CPD for teachers who are not at leadership level there is a huge proliferation of companies such as Capita and SSAT, and individuals as well as local authorities and universities. Little of this CPD is quality assured and most does not provide formal accreditation for teachers. While the NCTL is developing a modular course with pathways, the development of these courses and the quality assurance may become fragile. Moreover, the transformation of the NCTL into a government agency raises long-term questions about its independence. The CPD model of the Royal College of Surgeons is particularly attractive: the RCS does not solely deliver CPD but quality assures a variety of CPD and maintains a record of attendance for members. I also think that it is important that the standardisation and quality assurance of teachers' CPD is led by one institution. In the current void, many institutions are building their own courses, and creating confusion amongst teachers and school leaders.

A royal college should be responsible for setting teaching standards and expectations of professional behaviour at various points in a teacher's career. As a consequence, there should be some type of disciplinary arm that would be able to remove the professional membership of the College from individuals or to insist that they have further training during a period of suspension. This role lay with the Teaching Agency (and now the NCTL). However, following the demise of the General Teaching Council (GTC), there is now only one sanction, which is the removal of qualified teacher status (QTS). A royal college should have the power to insist on a period of re-training for individuals who have failed to meet the standards of the profession but who demonstrate the ability and determination to improve.

A royal college must not become an arm of the teaching trade unions. In practice, this was a particular challenge for the GTC where two teacher unions gained a level of control over it as a consequence of the pattern of elections to its council. As an observer at the GTC, I recall being appalled by some of the heavily unionised behaviour and attitudes displayed at the meetings. I recall a particular incident where confidential papers had been leaked to one union and the perpetrator blatantly stood up and said that he did this as his first loyalty was to his union. In what remains a heavily unionised profession, ensuring its independence will be a real challenge for a royal college. In the case of the GTC, the chair went to a member of the NUT on two successive occasions. One way to avoid this pitfall would be to award the chair of the royal college to an individual who did not have affiliation or contact with a union. The election process for both the chair and members would also need to be carefully managed so that it does not become dominated by the unions. Ultimately, the unions themselves would benefit from this distinct separation of roles.

One of the major challenges would be funding the Royal College of Teaching. The vast majority of teachers do pay union fees and very few teachers pay for their own CPD. It would be difficult to see why they would affiliate to a royal college unless there were significant benefits. Sadly, teachers are notoriously careful with their money as they have a constant perception that they are poorly paid. This is despite significant relative increases in salary over the last two decades. If we were starting in a different place at a different time, it would be possible to insist that teachers affiliate to a royal college in order to achieve QTS. I think this will be a huge hurdle to clear. I also do not think that the solution used with the GTC (where the government provided £33 into teachers' salaries to then be withdrawn by the GTC) provides a viable way forward. It is a great pity that the GTC did not develop in the same way as its equivalent in Scotland. I was a member of the GTC while working in Scotland. The Scottish GTC is the gatekeeper to the profession, awards QTS, manages some CPD and is responsible for disciplinary functions. The GTC in Scotland is held in high esteem by teachers and the public. It has never permitted itself to become influenced by one teaching union – although Scottish teachers are also highly unionised. This may have evolved as a consequence of the fact that it has always been the case in Scotland that teachers have to be graduates. The development of graduate teachers in England is comparatively recent, dating only from 1974. It would probably be worthwhile having a discussion with the Scottish GTC to investigate how they have achieved such status with the profession and the public.

In order to achieve buy-in from teachers, I think it would be sensible to carry out some sort of national survey first to see where teachers feel the gaps lie and also whether a royal college could fill this. I know that many school leaders are very concerned by the merger of the National College with the Teaching Agency to form the NCTL and, indeed, that this body is an executive agency within the Department for Education (DfE). The difficulty there is the size of this new organisation and the organic growth

decisions around pedagogy
and the content of courses
for students are being made
by civil servants who have
never taught. Teachers must
take control as they are the
individuals with experience
of how children learn and
how much content they
can manage at each stage

of the DfE's areas of responsibility. Will those organisations be able to manage such a wide diversity of tasks and development?

It is important that teachers take responsibility for the development of their own profession. There are constant complaints that they are being 'done-to' and yet there is a reluctance to take control of their own destiny. Decisions around pedagogy and the content of courses for students are being made by civil servants who have never taught. Teachers must take control as they are the individuals with experience of how children learn and how much content they can manage at each stage. It would therefore be important that the Royal College of Teaching had a research arm that looked at the development of curriculum and pedagogy and could present a balanced viewpoint to both the government and the public. I believe that many teachers would voluntarily give up their time to be actively involved in such development.

It is starting to feel as though many of the responsibilities that now fall under the NCTL should perhaps be devolved to a royal college. This may solve the problems of that institution becoming large and amorphous. As the remits of the National College and the Teaching Agency have merged, this is now a huge area of responsibility. It is possible that some tasks may be subsumed into others or even lost completely. However, as a Royal College of Teaching would be taking over some functions that currently lie with government, perhaps the government should consider grant-aiding for, say, an initial period of ten years.

The challenges facing a Royal College of Teaching are formidable. Government has extended its remit and competence in the fields of pedagogy, standards, leadership and discipline. Unions remain enormously influential not only in relation to terms and conditions of service but also in policy development and CPD. The economics of a royal college are daunting. And yet, the imperatives are considerable. The outcome is important. A properly constituted and led Royal College of Teaching could transform the professional landscape. It is a prize worth having.

Career progression and talent management

James Toop
Chief Executive, Teaching Leaders

Introduction

In 1997, McKinsey & Company coined the term 'the war for talent' as the name for their original research on talent management practices and beliefs. It described a phenomenon that many corporations were experiencing and the term has reverberated around the business world ever since. They claimed that as we moved from the industrial age to the information age, a company's value lies in its intangible assets, its intellectual capital and innovative ideas; in short, its talent. They surmised that 'better talent is what will separate the winning companies from the rest'.[1]

If talent management is about attracting and retaining the best individuals in a particular sector or organisation, then education is fighting a war for talent to attract the best individuals into the profession. Teach First is a prominent example of an initiative launched to increase the number of top graduates choosing teaching and encouraging career changers to move into the classroom. The successful media campaigns by the Teaching Agency have also been successful in raising the profile of teaching as a career path for graduates and young professionals, and the new School Direct model has added another entry route into teaching, driven and delivered by high performing schools. Given what we know about the impact of a good teacher on pupil achievement, this war for talent is a much more important one because it concerns the future education of the next generation.

Yet, as education starts to attract more top graduate and career changers into teaching, it raises the question of how the sector will retain these talented teachers once in the system. The recent House of Commons Education Select Committee report highlighted that the 'retention of teachers is low',[2] with only 52% of graduate teacher trainees remaining in education five years after qualifying. It states that 'wastage, in particular where it concerns those of the highest quality or in the most challenged schools, is clearly a cause for concern'. Furthermore, a 2005 report by Smithers and Robinson found that 'the more challenged secondary schools are more likely to lose teachers to other schools',[3] suggesting an internal war for talent if those teachers do remain in teaching.

The Select Committee's report suggests that the two key levers for retaining and developing talent within the system are professional development and career progression. David Weston addresses the case for more systematic, high quality continuing professional development (CPD) in his chapter, where the Royal College of Teaching could play an interesting role. However, while CPD allows teachers to progress and develop their *skills*, the societal, individual and sector-wide shifts occurring both within and outside education mean there is a need to focus on how teachers progress their *careers* as well: this could be a potential priority for a Royal College of Teaching. A focus on career progression could make a huge difference to the profession, raising its status and putting it on a par with law and medicine. It will help us with the ultimate challenge: to attract the best from other sectors, retain them when they are here, and accelerate their development to have the greatest impact on pupils.

a focus on career progression could make a huge difference to the profession, it will help us with the ultimate challenge: to attract the best from other sectors, retain them when they are here, and accelerate their development to have the greatest impact on pupils

Individual shifts and societal undercurrents

Profound shifts are happening in society across all sectors, which are turning old maxims on their head. The command and control structures are becoming flatter and matrixed, organisations are becoming more flexible with distributed leadership, information is more readily available and democratic, and communication is more informal. This organisational shift is symptomatic of the information and digital age, as well as the modern culture that many companies feel their employees will respond to. While this may not always be possible in schools as they are *in loco parentis*, a simple summary of how organisations have been changing more broadly is below.[4]

	The old way	The new way
Structures	Tall hierarchies Command and control	Flat matrix Lead and empower
Communication	Top down One channel, once	360 degrees Multiple channels
Power	Formal Hierarchy	Informal Networks
Work time	Standardised 8am-4pm	24/7, flexible
Staff	Compliance Salary and promotion	Commitment Recognition and status
Leadership	Hero	Distributed

The recent changes to structures and school autonomy within the education system leave schools well placed to take advantage of the new way. At a system level, teaching has always been a profession focused on commitment to mission rather than financial reward. Over the last decade leadership practices have moved to distributed models with wider senior leadership teams, and the recent growth of teaching schools and national leaders of education have increased networks and collaboration between schools. This leaves room at the top end to retain experienced heads as executive heads and leaders of academy chains, with more senior leaders progressing into headship to learn under them. Furthermore, schools have increasing levels of freedom, autonomy and flexibility to address the changing needs of their teachers and leaders through staffing structures and the reform to pay scales.

However, the expectations of individual employees and teachers have shifted too, with implications for how employers need to think about their staff. Teachers are increasingly looking for rapid promotion with the idea that performance in a role for two years is enough to be ready for the next step. They are more inclined to believe it is the employer's role to motivate them and find them opportunities, and are prepared to move if that is not fulfilled. They are more likely to be happy to transition out of education to gain experience and then return with an enhanced skill set. They also want performance to be recognised and rewarded.

This led McKinsey to suggest that employers should re-assess how they think about their staff. While adopting this way of thinking may go too far if taken literally (ie the organisation's goals should not become subservient in the focus on talent retention), it is indicative of a mindset shift, which is adapted for the education sector below.

	The old way	The new way
Talent mindset	Having good teachers is one of many important performance levers for the school	Having outstanding teachers at all levels is the key to raising achievement
Employee value proposition	Teachers work hard and make their way up the ladder	Teachers are here because they want to be and we have to keep it that way
Growing leaders	Development is training	Development happens through a series of challenging job experiences and candid, helpful coaching
	Development happens when you are lucky enough to have a good line manager	Development is crucial to performance and retention, and it can be institutionalised
Differentiation	Differentiation undermines teamwork	Recognise top performers, develop and nurture mid-performers, help lower performers or move them out

The gaps in education

While the education system is well placed in many regards, there are still a number of gaps which could threaten the education system as it moves forward.

Career pathways and structures

→ **Teaching still perceived as a career for life:** despite introductions such as Teach First, many individuals are put off the idea of teaching as a career for life. More flexible pathways in and out of the profession are required, and also recognition of the benefits of gaining experience from outside the classroom could bring in fresh talent and improve the practice of existing teachers.

→ **Leadership is the only strand for progression:** there is currently no career path unless you want to be a middle leader, senior leader or headteacher. This is especially important for teachers who want to keep improving their teaching and progress their careers while remaining in the classroom.

→ **Lack of structures and standards for progression:** as accountability for, and monitoring of, annual improvement in teaching quality resides at the level of individual schools, there is a lack of national consistency in minimal qualifications and standards around middle or senior leadership to recognise performance at that level. It takes 10,000 hours to master an activity so over a forty-year career; some structure to recognise progression and improvement could enhance motivation and give teachers a sense they are moving forward.

Increasing competition in the system

→ **Geographical challenges:** schools in rural and coastal areas struggle to attract and retain top talent due to their geography when compared to major urban areas. There is a risk that these areas will become increasingly isolated.

→ **School groups and clusters increasing internal levels of competition:** as groups and clusters of schools form, they have a significant advantage in attracting, progressing and retaining talent because they have the scale to offer secondments and moves staff between schools with integrated career and development pathways to grow their own leaders. Individual schools will find this an increasing challenge to compete with.

Awareness and innovation

→ **Lack of creativity in development opportunities:** schools typically lack the awareness and knowledge of innovative ways to develop and retain staff. Ideas such as secondments and research sabbaticals are not widespread and are seen as risks. More innovation and testing could have a huge impact on teacher quality and retention.

→ **Visibility of new roles/opportunities:** there is no central place where teachers can get information to take control of their careers. A central hub to find new roles, development opportunities and qualifications would have an impact on motivation and progression.

Solutions and emerging models

Education has a real need to focus on these gaps to ensure we continue to attract and manage our talent effectively. There is a need for more formal structures around career progression, particularly in individual schools in more isolated areas, which may not be able to benefit from some of the larger scale solutions offered by groups of schools. However, this has to be balanced against the flexibility of an increasingly autonomous school system with the ability to innovate and create new pathways and opportunities.

Four models below suggest some potential solutions which could be introduced, replicated or adopted.

1. National career pathway structure: Singapore

In Singapore, teachers elect to follow one of three career pathways (see figure, opposite). This career structure allows all teachers to pursue their own particular interests and strengths, whether in pedagogy, leadership or an area of specialism such as behaviour management or curriculum development.

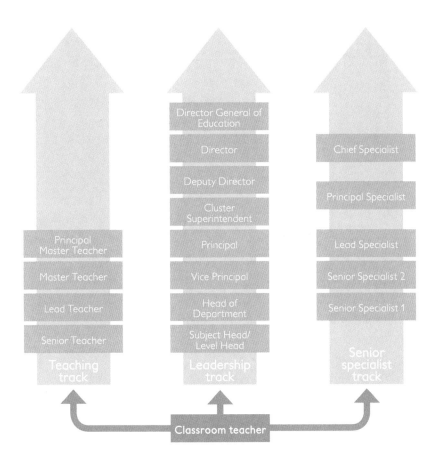

Director General of Education

Director

Chief Specialist

Deputy Director

Principal Specialist

Cluster Superintendent

Principal Master Teacher

Principal

Lead Specialist

Master Teacher

Vice Principal

Senior Specialist 2

Lead Teacher

Head of Department

Senior Specialist 1

Senior Teacher

Subject Head/ Level Head

Teaching track

Leadership track

Senior specialist track

Classroom teacher

2. Informal career pathways through aligned professional development programmes: Teach First, Teaching Leaders, Future Leaders

Three innovative, selective, non-profits, Teach First, Teaching Leaders and Future Leaders share a common mission to address educational disadvantage by developing outstanding leaders in schools in challenging contexts. Their shared approach has created an informal career structure for leaders who frequently move on and progress through the three programmes.

3. Leveraged group-wide/geographic innovation: academy chain bespoke career paths

Academy groups and schools clustered geographically are creating their own career structures in the same way that a corporate professional services firm might. This includes core and fast-track training at all levels within initial teacher training through Schools Direct, which identifies high potentials from initial recruitment and aims to retain them within the group for their career. The key difference is that the scale of the group allows it to facilitate secondments and move staff between schools depending on where the need or development opportunities lie.

4. In-school knowledge and mindset development to manage individuals: McKinsey

McKinsey provided individual corporations with helpful frameworks and ideas to develop career paths. At the heart were the five elements of a successful talent formula:

→ **Talent mindset at all levels:** all leaders make talent identification and development a key part of their role. They hold themselves accountable for the strength of the talent pool.

→ **Create a winning employee value proposition:** create a reason for employees to come and work for the organisation that is unique and compelling.

→ **Recruit great talent continuously:** great organisations are always on the search for talent and look in new ways and places to find it. They recognise the increasingly competitive landscape for talent.

→ **Grow great leaders:** most organisations leave much potential undeveloped. Growing leaders can be both formal and informal, but this growth must exist in the organisation as a core focus, not as an added extra.

→ **Differentiate and affirm:** organisations often treat all employees the same, but leading organisations conduct objective assessments of staff and reward and invest in their talent.

a Royal College of Teaching could provide the thought-leadership and validation from a member organisation whilst leaving teachers and schools with the option of adopting or adapting

The potential role of a Royal College of Teaching

A Royal College of Teaching could be well placed to develop ideas to address some of these challenges, providing national coherence and oversight whilst still leaving schools with the freedom to adopt them or develop their own. It could provide the thought-leadership and validation from a member organisation whilst leaving teachers and schools with the option of adopting or adapting. Some areas a Royal College of Teaching might develop include:

→ **Map career pathways and high quality accreditation routes for teachers and specialists:** for teachers who do not want to pursue the leadership route, this would give a sense of annual progression and the opportunity to meet peer-validated accreditation which increase motivation

→ **Integrate leadership pathway with existing professional development programmes:** work with organisations such as Teach First, Teaching Leaders and Future Leaders to establish wider informal career pathways for teachers through professional development opportunities linked to career transition points.

→ **Become a knowledge hub and develop expertise around career progression:** train and advise school leaders on how to implement and develop career pathways for teachers. This could also include sharing local knowledge.

→ **Hold central repository of jobs and development opportunities:** provide a central point for all teachers to find new roles and opportunities, searchable by role and geography, which would provide continuity and a national overview for teachers.

→ **Promote and raise the status of teaching to demonstrate career progression:** the presence of a Royal College of Teaching would do much to raise the status of the profession, but it could take a clear stand to support the National College for Teaching and Leadership's work to attract new teachers.

Closing remarks

Education has been fighting its own war for talent to attract, retain and develop the best teachers from other sectors for a decade and is now bringing in the best generation of teachers ever. As the quality of teachers rises and schools become more autonomous, there is the potential for an internal war for talent. Whatever happens, a focus for career progression and talent management is a key role for a Royal College of Teaching to explore.

Notes

1. Michaels E, Handfield-Jones H and Axelrod A. *The War for Talent.* Boston: Harvard Business Press; 2001.

2. House of Commons Education Committee. *Great teachers: attracting, training and retaining the best.* London: The Stationery Office Limited; 2011.

3. Smithers A and Robinson P. *Teacher Turnover, Wastage and Movements between Schools.* Research Report RR640. Nottingham: Department for Education and Skills; 2005.

4. Owen J. *The death of modern management: how to lead in the new world disorder.* Hoboken: Wiley; 2009.

5. Adapted from Michaels, *The War for Talent.*

Lessons from
Teach First

James Westhead
Executive Director of External Relations, Teach First,
and former Education Correspondent, BBC

Introduction

Great teaching and leadership in schools are among the most powerful forces for social change. Indeed, this is why Teach First was created ten years ago – to try to divert some of the steady flow of Britain's leadership talent away from seductively well-paid jobs in banking, law and accountancy and into our most disadvantaged communities where it is most needed. As a result, today Britain's top graduates are not merely thinking about teaching: they are actively, even fiercely, competing for the privilege of teaching in the poorest areas of the country through Teach First and, beyond that, many are staying for the long term. The bad news is that simply getting talent into the profession – through whichever route – is nowhere near enough. To sustain school and system improvement, we need to nurture and develop teaching talent by creating a culture of continuing professional development where teachers share their expertise, learn from one another and strive for excellence. That is why Teach First supports the proposal for a Royal College of Teaching and believes that, if done well, it will have an important role to play in the next stage of improvement for our education system.

From our experience, however, the journey towards a Royal College of Teaching won't be easy and it will face many obstacles. So, this article will try to share some of the lessons Teach First learned along the way when creating a new organisation to bring new ideas and change to education. Many will doubt the idea and only a few will be sufficiently strong believers to act, so one of the biggest obstacles for any genuinely new initiative is how to move from concept to reality. How do you build sufficient support and momentum to get over that initial hurdle to turn ideas into action? Even when launched, a Royal College of Teaching – like Teach First – will need to build a brand, a reputation, an image and a reality that is unique, recognised and respected. Teach First has tried to do this and is still trying. And, finally, the College will need to build a community of teachers committed to its vision and connected to each other – much as Teach First has sought to build a movement of ambassadors (graduates of our two-year leadership development programme) with a life-long commitment to addressing educational disadvantage.

From concept to reality

A decade ago, when the founder of Teach First – Brett Wigdortz OBE – explained the concept to the head of careers at one of our top universities, the academic chuckled indulgently and explained, 'I'm very sorry but our sort of people will never want to work in those sort of schools. They want something with more prestige.' This was just one of many obstacles to the prospect of a highly selective two year leadership development programme bringing the best graduates to teach in the most challenging schools. Other 'impossible' barriers were that there was no way that the graduates could be trained to teach on the job, schools would never want to hire teachers who were initially unqualified, where the money would come from, and that government and business would never support or fund the idea. Most of all, it would require an unprecedented degree of cooperation and coordination between schools, teacher trainers, graduates, unions, businesses and government and this would never happen. At several points in the early stages it seemed that Teach First would remain a nice idea that couldn't become reality.

However, there were some social and political tectonic plates that were shifting in its favour and a unique cocktail of people and circumstances to help make it happen. At that time, school performance overall was improving but there was growing concern about the long tail of underperforming secondary schools and the achievement gap for young people from low income backgrounds. Tony Blair's government had a new focus on education and was on the lookout for new ideas to help, so the timing was right. The economy was booming but employment patterns were shifting. Graduates were no longer looking for a job for life – so-called 'Generation Y' graduates were looking for more than mere money from a career. Research showed they wanted personal development, leadership, challenge and ultimately a more flexible, varied portfolio career. This was not enough, so, at the same time, Brett was busy building a small group of passionate champions from every sector – government, those in teacher training, headteachers, teaching unions and the business world. This was the crucial stage where the concept might well have failed. The idea and its potential caught the imagination of a small number of key leaders in

One of the biggest lessons learnt over the years has been the importance of not compromising on quality

every sector. These were the people who could overcome the barriers. A handful of business leaders gave seed funding, some senior government officials helped to change rules and regulations and eventually secure official support, forward-thinking teacher-trainers within universities helped design training programmes that worked, headteachers and union leaders lent their advice and critical public support. The crucial ingredient in the cocktail, though, was leadership. Brett may have had the idea and the determination but he also knew that it was others who would have to make it happen and his job was to find them and inspire them with his vision for change. Similarly, a Royal College of Teaching will require leadership and some committed and influential champions to move from concept to reality.

Building a brand

We needed a brand that would appeal to the nation's best graduates; a brand that could compete with the biggest city firms and attract the greatest talent. Our aim was to change the nature of conversations on campus. Teach First should be so prestigious that final year students would be at least as jealous of their colleagues who secured a place on Teach First as they would be of those who got jobs with blue-chip employers. We had to change perceptions. Teaching in a school in challenging circumstances couldn't just become slightly more prestigious than before – it had to become the most prestigious and well-thought-of graduate job out there. This was about radical, not gradual, change. So the original 'value proposition' sought to appeal to both the head and the heart: 'gain skills and an inside track' and 'make a difference'. At the same time, we aimed to present an old profession – teaching – through a new prism, which for us was leadership.

One of the biggest lessons learnt over the years has been the importance of not compromising on quality. So, even in the first year when we had 1,000 applicants for 200 places, we didn't fill all the places because we were determined to keep the quality high. It was a difficult decision but proved right in the long term as excellence has followed excellence and, over the years, as numbers have grown so has the quality of our participants. If we had taken the easy way at times and reduced standards, it is unlikely we would have been able to build our reputation and brand to get to this stage. The result has been a constant presence in the top ten of the *The Times'* Top 100 league table of most prestigious graduate employers – we are currently in fourth place. This year, we will become Britain's largest graduate recruiter for the first time with more than 8,000 applicants for 1,250 places ,including applications from a staggering 10% of all final-year students at Oxford and Cambridge universities.

As we have grown so the brand has evolved. At its heart, Teach First has always been about changing the lives of the least advantaged children, but this has not always been at the forefront. Initially, as we sought to compete with big city firms that we didn't communicate so clearly the 'why', focusing instead on the 'what' and the 'how'. This has led to some misconceptions, in particular that we are a government-run elite teaching route, rather than a charity tackling educational disadvantage. Over the years, as the brand has become more established, we have been able to more clearly articulate the purpose of Teach First and our vision that no child's educational success should be limited by their socio-economic background. For the College, the challenge around building the brand will be similar but also different. Instead of changing the perception of students towards teaching, the College's challenge may be to change the perception of teachers themselves towards their own profession. To do that, it will need to focus closely on its value proposition and be very clear about what it can offer, not just to individual teachers, but to the whole education system and wider society. Creating an identity that appeals to the breadth of audiences will be crucial, and defining a clear purpose, which is easy to communicate, will be a good starting point.

Building a community

From the beginning, Teach First has been much more than a teacher training organisation. It has sought to build a community or a movement of individuals with a life-long commitment to addressing educational disadvantage and to helping realise our shared vision for children. Initially, we saw the core of this community as the alumni of the programme – Teach First ambassadors. The majority remain in schools, with around two-thirds staying in teaching beyond the two-year programme. Teach First seeks to connect, engage and equip this growing number of ambassadors both inside and outside the classroom to address the problem of educational disadvantage in whatever way they can. In addition, we have realised that we need to build an even wider community, including the more than 500 schools we work with, 14 university training partners and more than 60 corporate business supporters.

If the College is to succeed as a professional body, it too will need to inspire a community of teachers committed to the shared vision and values of the College – and united by a purpose which includes but extends beyond self-interest to excellence, constant learning, and improvement. This takes years of hard work and a very clear strategy.

Teach First has advantages. We carefully select our recruits according to tough criteria around leadership, teaching potential and commitment to addressing disadvantage so they perhaps inevitably feel a connection. Our teachers then share the intense bonding experience of their initial six week residential Summer Institute, followed by two formative years in school on the leadership development programme. Nevertheless, we still work hard to find ways to help each Teach First cohort connect and bond so that they build the friendships and support networks that will sustain them through their time on the programme. Much of this comes down to communication. We have Facebook pages where cohorts can begin to connect with one another long before they even embark on the programme. Participants themselves go on to set up other, smaller groups based on their subject, region, or other factors – for instance, those who are career changers – and, last year, we launched our own community website where teachers come together online to ask questions, discuss opportunities and challenges, and share best practice.

Even with the training and support mechanisms provided by Teach First, teaching can be surprisingly isolating. Opportunities for teachers to connect and learn from each other need to be specifically created within schools or outside of school hours. So, groups of Teach First teachers across England and Wales are creating informal networks to share experiences and ways of working. For example, teachers in Yorkshire have set up monthly sessions to share best practice and enjoy social time together. In London, teachers have set up 'impact networks' – groups who bring professional challenges for discussion in a non-judgmental setting. These conversations are then uploaded to the community website where other teachers can comment on them.

Opportunities for teachers to connect and learn from each other need to be specifically created within schools or outside of school hours

Finally, Teach First seeks to support the continuing professional development of its ambassadors through access to training and opportunities. Every participant has the opportunity to embark on a Masters in Educational Leadership and to access high-quality coaching opportunities, internships, brokered support, such as job swaps and secondments, and CPD events. We also offer information, advice and guidance on wider careers that will enable ambassadors to continue to tackle educational disadvantage, access to networks and to other development programmes, such as Teaching Leaders and Future Leaders.

Conclusion

Starting up any new organisation is a challenge. Starting one within an education system that faces at once significant and fundamental change, and at the same time has deep-seated traditions, is no mean feat. Teach First hasn't always got it right but we hope that in this chapter we have been able to share some of our lessons learnt that will be helpful to the Royal College of Teaching as it emerges. Like many other teachers, Teach First teachers are innovators, keen to share and keen to learn. Having access to, and being a member of, an even wider network that facilitates this, ultimately to the benefit of the pupils we are all working for, is an exciting prospect.

What's in it for the unions?

Christine Blower
General Secretary, National Union of Teachers (NUT)

Chris Keates
General Secretary, National Association of
Schoolmasters Union of Women Teachers (NASUWT)

Dr Mary Bousted
General Secretary, Association of Teachers and
Lecturers (ATL)

Deborah Lawson
General Secretary, Voice

Russell Hobby
General Secretary, National Association of Head
Teachers (NAHT)

Brian Lightman
General Secretary, Association of School and College
Leaders (ASCL)

Christine Blower

Morale in the teaching profession is at dangerously low levels. This is reflected starkly in the results of an NUT-commissioned YouGov survey that was published at the turn of 2013. This saw more than half (55%) of teachers describe their morale as low or very low, an increase of 13% since teachers were asked the same question in April 2012. The later survey also found 69% of teachers reporting a decline in their morale since the last general election.

In this context, it is hardly surprising that there has been renewed interest in the establishment of a College of Teaching to add its voice to those of the NUT and other unions, calling for renewed faith in and promotion of the professional autonomy of teachers.

At a preliminary meeting convened by the Prince's Teaching Institute in September 2012, there was broad agreement that such a body could make a significant contribution to the interests of the teaching profession and the education system by promoting professional development, encouraging the use of evidence to inform education policy and assisting with the translation of research into classroom practice. The NUT was also happy that a number of participants suggested that the word 'royal' should be dropped.

More contentious were questions such as whether registration should be compulsory. Linked to that is the vexed question of the charging of fees, particularly at a time when teachers are suffering financially on so many fronts, and appreciation that the College's success would depend upon participation being attractive to teachers. Also important is a recognition of the history of representation of the profession through the teacher organisations, and for the College to find a meaningful and unique role even though there may be interests and views in common.

Should the College work toward having a regulatory function? As thinking around the College's remit is developed and refined, it will be interesting to consider whether it could embody the principle of teacher self-regulation, with the task of regulatory functions being carried out by those who have the specialised knowledge necessary to do the job.

The answers to these questions will be well served by detailed discussion and consultation. The NUT believes that the College must have two underlying objectives. Firstly, the College should use every opportunity to emphasise the professionalism of teachers. In particular, it should advocate the ability of teachers to exercise their professional judgement in teaching and learning activities and the need for assessment and school accountability mechanisms to be based on trust in the profession.

Secondly, it should advocate for a career-long entitlement to high quality professional learning opportunities for all teachers, including supply teachers. It is through an entitlement to continuing professional development, which is integral to a teacher's work and not additional to teachers' workloads, that teachers' enthusiasm and commitment to teaching can be enhanced. Such an approach would also reduce the still unacceptably high rate of teacher turnover and loss to the profession.

The NUT has a long history of campaigning for professional autonomy. We are keen to discuss these questions and more and to participate in exploratory steps towards a College of Teaching.

Chris Keates

Teacher professionalism matters, and is at the heart of debates about the establishment of a Royal College of Teaching because quality public education relies upon the quality of the workforce in schools and throughout the public services. Governments need to demonstrate their commitment to teachers in words and in deeds, and by conferring professional rights on teachers that affirm the professional status of their and which are guaranteed across all public education settings.

The report of the OECD to the inaugural International Summit on the Teaching Profession, published in 2011, set out a clear responsibility for government to commit to establishing an education system that recognises and develops teachers as professionals. A world class school system cannot be sustained where there is no guarantee of quality professionals working in every school. A national framework of professional requirements and standards, underpinned by a framework of professional terms and conditions of service, including a contractual entitlement to professional development and training, is critical to ensuring quality for all children and young people.

This is a well-established principle in other professions, such as medicine, accountancy and law, where common qualification and practice standards, backed by effective regulatory arrangements, ensure that the highest levels of practice are promoted and sustained, providing an assurance of quality for the users of professionally staffed services.

The de-professionalisation of teaching, resulting from the policy agenda of the coalition government, must therefore represent a matter of profound concern for all those with a stake in ensuring that the highest standards of educational provision continue to be established in our schools. The removal of the requirement for teachers in state-funded schools to possess Qualified Teacher Status, considered alongside the effective deregulation of teaching, serve to highlight the current government's conceptualisation of teaching as a 'craft', learned simply through mimicking the practice of others, rather than as a complex professional activity.

These considerations emphasise the fact that meaningful work to establish a Royal College of Teaching cannot precede action to place teaching on an appropriately regulated, professional footing in all sectors, both state-funded and independent. Rather than enhance the status of the profession, attempts to establish a royal college without dealing with the regulation and accreditation of teaching would simply serve to diminish the standing of teaching in comparison with other professions.

In the absence of appropriate government regulation, and where professional autonomy is extended, there need to exist clear, professionally derived codes of conduct to regulate professional behaviours and practice, overseen by an appropriate regulatory body such as a general teaching council or equivalent.

The NASUWT has argued consistently for such a body, citing equivalents in medicine and law. The body should be the standard-bearer for teacher quality and excellence and command the support of the teaching profession. In such circumstances, a royal college could then begin to make a contribution to enhancing the professional status of teaching through, for example, ensuring that all teachers have access to the highest quality professional development and training opportunities.

Dr Mary Bousted

The Education Select Committee wants one. Michael Gove isn't sure but thinks it's OK as long as he doesn't have to pay for it. But before we decide whether a Royal College of Teaching is the answer, we have to look at the question.

Which, in my view, is: why is teacher morale so low? The evidence cannot be ignored. Survey results show clearly that too many teachers are not enjoying their work.

There can be many interrelated and complex reasons for low morale, which can include excessive workload, stress caused by inspection and target setting, and the frenzy of activity which characterises the current working day for teachers (who, lest we forget, cannot retreat to the office, decide upon their own work priorities and take some 'quiet time' – Year 9 awaits!).

But the biggest cause of low morale is lack of agency. Teachers, like members of any other profession, want to feel in control of key elements of their professional practice. Unfortunately, they are not.

The current coalition government has excelled itself in demonstrating the problem. The first legislative act of the coalition was its education bill, rushed through the House of Commons with unseemly haste. It comes to something, I think, when teachers are regarded by politicians as dangerous opponents.

the biggest cause of low morale is lack of agency. Teachers, like members of any other profession, want to feel in control of key elements of their professional practice. Unfortunately, they are not

The current government and its predecessors have, for the past forty years, driven a constant revolution in education policy. Each succeeding administration, keen to make its mark and widen its scope of influence has introduced legislation to control the education system. We are now at the end of the road of this approach. We have arrived at a place where too many teachers feel little or no agency and where matters which should be left to the teaching profession – matters which go to the heart of what it is to be a professional – are the subject of ministerial dictat. The curriculum, the qualifications which count, teaching and learning strategies, approaches to special education needs, teaching standards, and so much more – all are decided by politicians whose conclusions are fine for the sound and fury of the Westminster village but utterly unsuitable in raising standards of teaching and learning in our schools.

This is why ATL has concluded that the creation of an independent professional voice is needed; a place in which the profession can regain the ground on which it should stand. This is the job of the Royal College of Teaching.

Deborah Lawson

Morale within teaching is at a low point because of a lack of esteem within the profession and a decline in government and public respect for teachers. We would welcome any attempt to raise the status of teaching as a profession and restore public confidence and respect.

We had hoped that the General Teaching Council for England (GTC) would rise to this challenge. Unfortunately, it over-emphasised its regulatory functions and was seen by many teachers as an external imposition that lacked interest in their welfare.

An examination of GTC's failure is crucial in ensuring that any Royal College of Teaching is correctly founded.

It should be independent of government, owned and controlled by teachers, and open to teachers in all phases of education (nursery to tertiary) in both the public and private sectors.

We foresee many potential benefits of such an initiative. It would help to galvanise the profession, raise aspirations, motivation, standards

it would help to galvanise the profession, raise aspirations, motivation, standards and status, and provide a vehicle for promoting continuing professional development

and status, and provide a vehicle for promoting continuing professional development in subject knowledge and generic teaching skills, as well as the development of apposite dispositional and attitudinal aspects of being a professional teacher.

It could also act as an umbrella organisation, bringing together subject associations, phase associations, unions and other professional associations allied to teaching, and engage in research. We have three main concerns:

1. Relentless government intrusion into education over several decades has undermined and compromised teachers' professional autonomy, so, to build capacity for such an initiative, there would need to be active government promotion, support and brokering to bring together interested parties and facilitate the actions and dialogue needed to implement an appropriate scheme.

2. We are sceptical about the view that a Royal College of Teaching would ensure that 'politics is kept out of the classroom'. While such a college would champion the profession as a whole, rather than meddle in individuals' employment issues or in the collective terms and conditions of particular groups of teachers, much of what happens in the classroom is shaped by political decisions underpinned by statutory measures. Therefore, we would expect a Royal College of Teaching to engage in the political process by maintaining a dialogue with government and lobbying in matters of policy and legislation (especially curriculum, assessment and initial teacher training).

3. We assume that a Royal College of Teaching would need to levy fees for it to function. In the current climate, many teachers would not be able to afford the membership fees charged by some of the established royal colleges, such as the Royal College of Surgeons, whose members' salaries are far in excess of what teachers earn. There would, therefore, need to be an element of 'pump-priming' or a significant increase in teachers' economic position (which has been exacerbated by the current pay freeze); otherwise, the College would struggle to attract members.

We are keen to participate in constructive dialogue and want to be able to promote a viable scheme to our members.

Russell Hobby

Professionalism is like trust. Trust cannot be asserted; it is earned by being trustworthy. Similarly, professionalism isn't a claim; it is earned by being professional. While I'm running with analogies, I'd also suggest that politicians are like nature. No, not necessarily unpredictable and dangerous: in the fact that they abhor a vacuum. If we leave a vacuum – by not addressing the difficult questions, for example – they will fill it for us.

NAHT therefore supports the concept of a Royal College of Teaching as a vehicle to recognise the professionalism of teachers and to reduce destructive political interference in the education system by taking ownership of standards. I can think of few better projects to raise the standing of teachers and improve working conditions over the long term.

Comparisons with the health sector are often rejected but I think they are also often apt. Professionalism means rooting practice in evidence, even when the messages are challenging, so we need a reliable source of evidence, free from distortion. It means holding and policing high standards for ourselves. It means a code of conduct that recognises the trust society places in us and its vulnerability to our choices.

I don't think medicine holds all the answers, however. Teachers will need to invent their own model of professionalism that recognises the partnership they have with parents and their leadership role in the community. It must be a collaborative rather than an authoritarian professionalism. And I think we also need to be clear that professionalism a Royal College of Teaching is a vehicle to recognise the professionalism of teachers and to reduce destructive political interference in the education system by taking ownership of standards doesn't mean being left alone. It means being trusted to use your skills and talent to solve challenges for which there are no easy answers. That doesn't mean that 'anything goes' or that the work is not accountable.

This is an exciting prospect but it has obstacles to overcome. We need to make an honest appraisal of the trajectory of the General Teaching Council, for a start. How will the new College be funded? What powers will it have? How independent is it? What is the relationship with the trade unions?

The College cannot succeed without the engagement – indeed, ownership – of teachers themselves. I believe that, with the right assurances and boundaries in terms of roles, this is something that teaching unions can and should embrace. But politicians will need to earn their trust too during the process of creation.

Brian Lightman

ASCL has always believed that teachers, like other professionals, need an independent professional body. For many years we campaigned for a General Teaching Council and, while we would have strongly supported significant changes to the remit and operation of the now defunct General Teaching Council for England, we viewed its abolition as a retrograde step. In ASCL's view, a high status profession would display the following six characteristics:

1. It would be self-regulating to exacting standards, attractive and oversubscribed, bringing in the highest quality of entrants in terms of qualifications and skills.

the greatest challenge will be to win the hearts and minds of the teaching profession

2. It would promote, develop and champion the very best evidence-based practice in subject, knowledge, pedagogy and assessment.
3. It would be in control of professional duties such as curriculum planning, methodology and in-service training, underpinned by a rigorous qualifications system to promote attractive career progression for the best teachers.
4. It would maintain, as part of rigorous self-regulation as well as professional reflection, an ethics committee to which issues of concern for the development, regulation or public understanding of teaching may be referred so that the profession may be guided in its moral purpose by the best ethical principles.
5. It would enjoy high levels of autonomy whilst embracing full acceptance of its public accountability with self-regulation.
6. It would be highly respected by public and government.

A Royal College of Teaching has the potential to be a major driver of these characteristics, setting and regulating the highest professional standards itself. In an increasingly fragmented and autonomous education system, there is a risk that wide variations in the quality of provision can develop without some kind of coherent framework of professional standards and expectations. It is for this reason that the movement towards the establishment of such a body is growing and that it has ASCL's support.

Nevertheless, there is one vitally important caveat: this is not something that can be imposed on the profession by government or by any other constituency or rushed into existence. While the key to its success will be the broadest support from the full spectrum of representative organisations, it will have to be truly independent.

The greatest challenge will be to win the hearts and minds of the teaching profession, who have an enormous amount to gain from having their own professional body. This would enhance their professional status by setting out a sustainable, long-term vision for the development of the profession and would provide them with a much-needed cushion from short term political considerations driven by the electoral cycle.

The time is now right for this idea to be debated by the profession.

A view from the subject associations

Ian McNeilly

Director, National Association for the Teaching of English

Dr John Steers

Chair, Council for Subject Associations

It is a universally held truth that education is of vital importance. It is also something that is fundamental to humanity, whatever your culture, creed or location. Acknowledging education's eternal value, one might be forgiven for assuming that many of the basic, organisational systems to allow it to thrive are not only in place but have been so for centuries.

This is not the case. It is utterly bewildering how a profession as vitally important as teaching still does not have a single, effective body that encourages and advances good practice in education, in England at least. It is very much to the sector's detriment – and to the detriment of both the practitioners and the pupils they teach.

Is teaching less worthy of having such a body than those professions which do? Not only do several other professions have a royal college or its equivalent body, but in many it would be unthinkable not to be a member. It is an honour that those practitioners have worked towards, and are rightly proud of. Not so with teaching. Yet.

The General Teaching Council for England (GTC) was imposed on teachers via the Teaching and Higher Education Act of 1998. Its function was regulatory but, putting this to one side, it also attempted initiatives to try and encourage teachers to develop professionally. It failed to do so, with any noticeable effect. The GTC closed in March 2012.

Present long before the GTC came (and still here after it went) are the many organisations which, as a group, constitute the *de facto* professional body for teaching and teachers: the subject associations.

Subject associations are normally membership organisations, often registered charities, whose mission is to further the teaching and learning of a specific subject or area of a subject in schools. They are independent of government, though often share a number of objectives. All subject associations share the unifying concept that they are interested in promoting quality in education and believe that this is done by supporting teachers and recognising and enhancing subject specialism.

Not only this, membership of a subject association is incredibly cost-effective, which is more crucial than ever in this current time of austerity.

When the present government launched its policy of the 'Big Society' in May 2010, the stated intention was 'to create a climate that empowers local people and communities, building a big society that will take power away from politicians and give it to people'. This is what subject associations have been doing for the teaching community for decades. How have they met this challenge?

Not all subject associations will do all of the following. Some will, and some will do more.

Provision of professional periodicals

Subject associations publish specialist periodicals, written mainly by members, for members. The content will be varied but will almost always include insights from practising teachers on what works for them – and what doesn't. High level quality assurance of resources and pedagogical strategies, while a vital, basic requirement for any teacher, is not as common as one might believe.

Another purpose served by the periodicals is to help teachers negotiate their way through the constant tinkering experienced in our sector. The saying 'the only thing that is constant is change' firmly applies to education; it is a Sisyphean task to keep updated with changes affecting teaching and the collaborative endeavour of subject association staff and members saves individuals a huge amount of time, and the forewarning can lessen the stress to which the changes sometimes lead.

Opportunities for professional development

While it has become more difficult to release teachers from school for a whole host of reasons, most subject associations feel duty bound to offer face-to-face professional development, as its value is unquestionable. Remote, visual communication is used with increasing frequency yet subject association research shows that one of the things most valued by teachers is the opportunity to convene in person and share ideas with their peers. There are fewer and fewer opportunities to do this these days, and the worry is that schools and their teachers will become less and less accustomed to updating their knowledge and skills this way. One could argue that some institutions and individuals are even subconsciously complicit in this, given these financially straitened times.

Subject association continuing professional development (CPD) courses are all quality assured and are invariably hosted by leading practitioners in their field – which is why they are members of their subject associations in the first place.

further education teachers who have to do a required amount of professional development annually to keep QTLS status. Why not the same for school teachers and QTS, one asks?

a Royal College of Teaching, underpinned by subject associations among others, would be a formidable organisation. It could provide the bedrock for subject teaching and expertise, a shared destination for accumulated knowledge, enabling subject associations to be more than the sum of their parts

They are also incredibly cost-effective; for a similar price as one might pay to attend a single day 'chalk and talk' input from a commercial provider, one can often attend a fully residential weekend at a subject-association event.

Members of some other professions are duty-bound to complete a certain amount of CPD hours per year; otherwise their fitness to practise is questioned. Indeed, this is the case with further education teachers who have to do a required amount of professional development annually to keep Qualified Teacher Learning and Skills (QTLS) status. Why not the same for school teachers and Qualified Teacher Status (QTS), one asks?

This is something that teaching as a profession should embrace – not resist – and a Royal College of Teaching could be the organisation to lead on this area. The potential benefits for teachers and their students of implementing such a self-evidently positive policy as this should not be underestimated.

Undertaking and disseminating research

Most people acknowledge that research evidence should inform practice, and subject associations have a great tradition in this area. A significant amount of educational research is undertaken either under the auspices of subject associations or by their members as individuals. The results are then distributed via a number of channels; many subject associations have their own academic journals, some of which are highly respected internationally with wide circulation. This serves an important function in subject communities.

Giving subjects a national voice

Subject associations offer expertise and experience in their areas and are regularly called upon by successive administrations to take part in consultations on the curriculum and related issues. When teachers are affected by change, unions speak up for them. But when subjects are affected, who is there to make sure they are heard?

This is a vital role for subject associations. For example, a theatre company was recently told by a Department for Education representative that drama wasn't a school subject but more a matter of pedagogy. This appears not only to be completely arbitrary but also simply untrue. Therefore, National Drama has made its voice heard and the subject association community has rallied round to support. A Royal College of Teaching would be a formidable and necessary voice in circumstances like these.

A Royal College of Teaching: making subject associations stronger

While appreciating the great work done by individual subject associations, their efforts would, at times, have been far more effective and productive had they worked either with other associations within the same subject (yes, there is sometimes more than one association per subject) or associations from different subject areas. This has happened occasionally but nowhere near as much as it should have done. It is a failing of the subject association movement that little genuine, enduring collaboration has taken place.

The Council for Subject Associations (CfSA) was founded in 2007 and it has been a valuable platform for exchanging ideas and concerns between individual groups. The CfSA has responded to all recent 'consultations' and the input has been excellent and agreement easier to obtain than might be expected. But, as a small voluntary body, it hasn't yet entirely fulfilled its promise of being the single voice subjects might benefit from.

A Royal College of Teaching, underpinned by subject associations among others, would be a formidable organisation. It could provide the bedrock for subject teaching and expertise, a shared destination for accumulated knowledge, enabling subject associations to be more than the sum of their parts, and integral to the very existence of a teaching profession. Imagine the knowledge, experience and enthusiasm that would be brought to a single organisation by more than thirty subject associations, with their wealth of expertise?

There can be no doubt that many subject association members may view a Royal College of Teaching as a potential threat to their continued existence. Their worries are not unfounded, which is why payment towards membership of a Royal College of Teaching absolutely must include an appropriate levy for recognised subject associations. By becoming a member of the Royal College of Teaching, any practitioner could nominate an established subject association of their choice, from which to receive the benefits described above.

Payment, of course, will be a sticking point for teachers and this is something which requires a cultural shift within the profession. Union membership is on the increase. Teachers are prepared to pay for something they see as directly relevant and important to them. This is what the Royal College of Teaching must be: an organisation of such quality and gravitas that to become a member is regarded as an honour and a privilege. Qualified teachers have earned the right to be thought of as high level professionals and there should be no sense of apology that individuals have to pay towards their own status and development, as other professionals habitually do.

Education is too important to be ideologically driven, and it is battered too often by the whims of whichever political administration passes through. Policy needs to be evidence-based and subject to genuine consultation. Politicians are transient; teachers and subject associations are there when the Secretary of State comes and are still there when he or she goes. A Royal College of Teaching would be an opportunity to begin to shift education and the considerable expertise and professionalism therein away from Westminster and Whitehall back into the hands of the profession itself.

Case study: the creation of the College of Emergency Medicine

Dr Ruth Brown
Vice President, College of Emergency Medicine

Summary

This case study describes the creation of the College of Emergency Medicine from the College (previously known as faculty) and British Association for Emergency Medicine. Though the analogy to any future Royal College of Teaching will only apply to a point, the process of establishing a modern professional body in the royal college mould is the same. To achieve royal college status, any potential professional body would have to go through these three key stages:

1. Establishing a need for an organisation which is distinctive in terms of the professional area it is to cover. In the case of the College of Emergency Medicine, there was a need to justify that it was sufficiently different from other forms of medicine to require its own body. This can be set up as a charity and or company limited by guarantee.

2. Incorporation of the organisation by Royal Charter. It must be emphasised that this does not make the organisation a royal college – at this stage it is only a college. The Royal Charter has to be approved by the Privy Council.

3. The addition of the 'Royal' to the name. This is a further step which again involves the Privy Council but also the explicit permission of the Queen. The College of Emergency Medicine has not yet done this.

The process

The College of Emergency Medicine was graciously granted a Royal Charter in 2008 having been created from the merging of two organisations that related to emergency medicine. Emergency Medicine has developed as a specialist branch of hospital medicine over the last sixty years, the first consultant in emergency medicine being appointed in 1952. However, the specialty as it is now really only developed as recently as 1972 when it was originally recognised as a specialty in the UK, first recognised training programmes in 1978 and the first professional examination in 1996.

   The British Association for Emergency Medicine (a charity) developed in 1967 as a society of physicians who worked in A&Es (or casualty as it was called then) and was first named the Casualty Surgeons Association. The purpose of the association was to support the development of the specialty – in research and in setting standards of professional practice or care for patients.

It was in 1983 that it was recognised that doctors working in emergency medicine may need different skills to those working in surgery or medicine in hospitals, and the first A&E specific exam was developed in Edinburgh by A&E doctors working with the Royal College of Surgeons of Edinburgh. This was followed in 1996, after the formation of the Faculty of Accident and Emergency Medicine (another charity), by an exam designed to test the final skills needed to be a consultant.

The faculty was primarily an academic body – formed with the support of six parent royal medical colleges (the Royal Colleges of Surgeons of England and of Edinburgh, of Physicians and Surgeons of Glasgow, of Physicians (London), and of Anaesthetists.) This 'parental' support was necessary to allow the formation of what was a new member of the medical professional colleges and therefore agreement had to be reached that it was necessary, and that the work of the faculty (and its members) was so different to other colleges as to warrant an additional organisation. The support given by the other medical royal colleges was invaluable over the course of the fifteen years of the faculty's life. The faculty developed both an academic portfolio (annual conferences, research grants, and academic training), and educational portfolio (training programmes, curriculum approved by the General Medical Council and examinations).

In 2005, having recognised that the work of the faculty was similar to that of a royal college, the members of the faculty voted to change the name to the College of Emergency Medicine. While this would not be with a Royal Charter, this still needed approval from the Academy of Medical Royal Colleges, the other medical royal colleges (including our 'parents') and the GMC, as well as the Department of Health. Agreement was reached that this was an appropriate name for the faculty given the wide range of activity, the maturity of our systems and processes and our ability to represent emergency medicine in the UK.

At the time of renaming, the then faculty also sought to become independent of our parent colleges. The proposal was that, since we were functioning autonomously, and the medical royal college representatives on our board were clearly advisory rather than authoritative, that we could continue to have their counsel but not to require their approval for our own business. This negotiation was satisfactorily completed after some lengthy discussions and on the 1st January 2006 we became the College of Emergency Medicine.

At this time, the College was a limited company – working under the legal constraints and requirements of company law. The members of the newly formed college felt that seeking Royal Charter was an important step, signifying our status, pre-eminence and stability. All royal colleges are established with a Royal Charter and as such are in themselves a legal entity (rather than a collection of individuals in a company). It should be noted that this did not convey a Royal appellation which is something that the College will still aspire to and one that requires Privy Council approval and consent from Her Majesty the Queen.

Why did we do it?

The drivers to first merge and then to seek Royal Charter were as follows:

→ Small new specialty – needed to establish ourselves with our peers in other specialties.
→ We had achieved a great deal in our two organisations in a short space of time and wished to have that formally recognised.
→ Two organisations both representing our interests meant dilution of effort and potential for confusion.
→ Double subscriptions for members was excessive.
→ Combined activities were easier to control and follow and financially better in terms of administrative costs.
→ Company law was not necessarily helpful for some of our activity.

How did we do it?

The initial request to members of both organisations to approve the move to merge was made at our annual general meetings. Such an important decision (which was known to cost quite a lot in terms of legal fees etc) had to be approved by members. There was some dissent and concern about losing the identity of one or other organisation but general approval.

the College has undertaken big projects on behalf of the membership that were made easier by being a single authoritative body

A clearly set out argument for merging, used by both organisations, was essential to ensure obvious consistency and shared vision by the officers of both organisations.

The negotiations with other organisations took many months and a lot of diplomacy. While much of the negotiation was undertaken by one or two people (with established skills and also credibility to outside organisations), no opportunity was lost in any discussions with relevant authorities to raise the possibility and to promote the idea of the College and eventual charter.

Operationally a merger board was formed with equal numbers of officer representatives to discuss the operational plans and make decisions. Regular updates to members were necessarily quite brief and vague until the go ahead was received. The work of the merger board in merging organisations and determining the new rules (charter and ordinances) was extensive (and expensive) as well as deciding how assets (bank accounts etc) were to be moved to the new organisation. In addition, there was an amount of discussion to be had about how activities would be governed and run. Inevitably, this took longer than wished for with the merger board being set up in late 2005 – a full three years before the final charter was received.

Was it worth it?

For the ordinary member, the only tangible benefit may be seen as fees that are controlled and only for one organisation. However, there is now a much clearer college structure – the committees and the work that the committees do is transparent and the benefits and privileges available are clearer. The College has undertaken big projects on behalf of the membership (including DH-sponsored e-learning, curriculum review, and a new training programme in emergency medicine) that were made easier by being a single authoritative body. Similarly, the development of 'peer' standing with the other royal colleges has increased the amount of access we have to the Academy of Medical Royal Colleges, and ensured we are the authority that other organisations turn to for advice on matters relating to emergency medicine. As a member of the International Federation for Emergency Medicine and the European Federation for Emergency Medicine, we are also respected and our standing valued by our overseas colleagues.

Lessons for a Royal College of Teaching

The application of the emergency medicine analogy will only apply so far to teaching, of course, but the following points are important in the establishment of any such royal college.

→ Ensure the members and potential members are behind you.

→ Take every opportunity to promote the organisation with everyone in every arena of authority.

→ Take it slowly – establish an organisation with resources and function, before applying for a royal charter.

→ Describe exactly what the benefit to the public will be of the establishment of the organisation – be sure you are focused but also leave it vague enough to add on functions in future without having to get a new charter.

→ Secure strong legal help – lawyers who understand what the organisation does but also understand the processes of Royal Charter – this will clearly cost money.

→ Ensure the membership will contribute to the vision for the College.

→ Ensure the College is unique – no other body should do what it does, or do it as well as it does.

Engineering: a case study in professional recognition

Jon Prichard
Chief Executive Officer, Engineering Council

History of professional standards in engineering

Up until the latter half of the 18th century, engineering was traditionally considered to be a military function, with public works being mainly constructed in order to further the influence of the realm. However, as global trade and commerce increased in importance, a need arose for civil (non-military) engineers to carry out works to support trade such as the construction of harbours and lighthouses. Methods and designs were developed using 'rules of thumb' and accidents and failures were common. In order to address this, the Society of Civil Engineers was established in 1771 to share and develop good practice. This society was subsequently renamed the Smeatonian Society, after John Smeaton, its founder, and the first person to call himself a 'civil engineer'.

In 1818, a group of younger engineers, who were not sufficiently eminent to join their seniors in the Smeatonian Society, established their own learned society, the Institution of Civil Engineers, which was the first professional engineering institution in the world. Under the leadership of Thomas Telford, their first president, the Institution was awarded a Royal Charter in 1828, which set out its objects as facilitating 'the acquirement of knowledge necessary in the civil engineering profession and for promoting mechanical philosophy'.

This object laid the blueprint for all subsequent professional engineering bodies, establishing two core functions: firstly, as a knowledge-standard-setting body for members; and secondly, as a forum for the exchange of good practice. As the Industrial Revolution in Britain took hold, then so did the proliferation of engineering institutions, including among others those for mechanical, electrical, mining, marine, and aeronautical engineering, each with its own Royal Charter. It is worth noting that in most commonwealth countries that subsequently established similar engineering institutions, they elected to establish a sole institution for all engineering disciplines (notably Australia, Canada, Hong Kong and New Zealand). This is partially due to the numbers of engineers who were practising in the respective countries and the related economies of scale. However, over time, some disciplines with fewer active members have found that their subject specialism does not receive adequate focus within a larger body to meet their particular knowledge needs.

One of the main benefits of the Industrial Revolution was the ability it created to mass produce goods at relatively low cost. However, a lack of control in terms of specification and quality meant that the market was awash with many different types of similar goods of variable quality. In terms of public procurement, this was highly inefficient. As a result the key chartered engineering institutions established the Engineering Standards Committee to address product proliferation. An early success for the Committee was a 90% reduction in the number of steel rail beams for trams from 75 different types to just six. As the committee's standardisation work developed to include a wider spectrum of goods and services, it was duly recognised with its own Royal Charter. It was then retitled in 1931 as the British Standards Institution (BSI). After the Second World War, the BSI became the UK's national standards body and also went on to help establish the International Standards Organisation (ISO) to promote and develop standards globally.

As Britain emerged from the 1950s post-war austerity, the chartered engineering institutions became concerned that there was a lack of conformity in professional engineering qualifications and that they should work together to address this variability by adopting a common threshold. By 1965, this joint initiative had formally come together as the Council of Engineering Institutions with its own Royal Charter, and for the first time a central register of chartered engineers, technician engineers (later called 'incorporated') and engineering technicians, with the post-nominals CEng, TEng and EngTech denoting an engineer's level of registration. In the early 1970s, the profession also adopted graduate entry for chartered-level qualifications, while still maintaining non-graduate routes for those progressing the 'hard way'. Such experiential routes have continued to be provided to this day, with much work have been undertaken by the institutions to develop methods to assess prior learning before candidates come forward for professional review interview by their peers.

During the late 1970s, as the UK experienced a decline in its manufacturing output, a school of thought developed that the engineering

this object laid the blueprint for all subsequent professional engineering bodies, establishing two core functions: firstly, as a knowledge-standard-setting body for members; and secondly, as a forum for the exchange of good practice

profession was not making the efficiency contribution to productivity that it should be when compared to Japan and the US. After much debate, a Committee of Inquiry was instigated under Sir Monty Finniston. Among the many issues that the inquiry considered, the key question that came to the fore was whether engineering should be self-regulating or be subject to statutory regulation. When the report *Engineering Our Future* was published by HMSO in 1980, self-regulation was favoured by Sir Keith Joseph, the then Secretary of State for Trade, as it was felt that statutory regulation would introduce a unnecessary level of bureaucracy and over prescription without significantly improving outcomes. However, statutory regulation was provided for in some areas of practice, where the risk to the public resulting from failure was deemed too onerous to be left to voluntary registration schemes (notably reservoirs, aviation and nuclear).

Thus the Engineering Council was created as a body incorporated by Royal Charter in 1981, inheriting the registers for chartered engineers, incorporated engineers and engineering technicians from the previous council. One of the key changes from this previous regime was the introduction of a common requirement for initial professional training and an enduring commitment to life-long education and training (subsequently called continuing professional development). Today, the Engineering Council licenses 36 professional engineering institutions to assess and nominate professional engineers and technicians to its registers, with over 230,000 individuals currently having demonstrated to their peers that they have attained the required competence and display the necessary commitment to practice. The institutions also fulfil their learned society role, by informing professional practice and enabling the professional development of their members, who number some 500,000 in total. The institutions further influence the work of an additional 1.2 million workers that the Office for National Statistics has classified as being in engineering roles.

Why self-regulate?

An interest in professional regulation is generally driven by a wish to protect consumers and society at large. The National Consumer Council has summarised the justifications for regulation as being when there is evidence of:

→ **Inadequate competition:** where suppliers, individually or collectively, dominate the market or make arrangements which reduce competition and consumer choice.

→ **Fraud, deception and oppressive marketing practices:** where suppliers take advantage of consumers in ways that are illegal or unfair.

→ **Imperfect information:** where the information essential to informed consumer choice is either completely unavailable, or false or misleading.

→ **Safety:** where there is risk of consumers using goods or services which may damage their health.

→ **Resolution of disputes and the pursuit of redress:** where easily accessible procedures are needed to make sure consumers can get a remedy for breaches of contract or other laws or codes.

→ **Externalities:** where there is a need to ensure that the costs of producing goods and services reflect all the consequences of their production (as with pollution).

→ **Social objectives:** where the market is unable to make socially desirable goods and services available for defined groups of consumers. Also, where an unregulated market is unlikely to achieve democratically desirable results relating to public order, taste and decency, and similar goals.

→ **Vulnerable consumers:** for example, those with weak bargaining power and children may need special or additional protection.

→ **Raising standards:** in a sector where businesses can gain a competitive advantage or where there are known to be problems with compliance with the law.

The justifications that particularly apply to engineering relate to 'safety' and 'raising standards'. Although 'raising standards' would be equally applicable to teaching, a secondary justification would be likely to be protecting 'vulnerable consumers'.

A spectrum of regulation exists within the wider professions, ranging from those with voluntary codes (such as engineering) through to those with statutory duties (such as architecture and law). Professional self-regulation is a regulatory model that enables government to exercise a level of control (the level being dependent on the relative positioning within the spectrum) over the practice of a profession and the services provided by its members. Self-regulation is based on the concept of an occupational group formally entering into an agreement with government to regulate the activities of its members. In the UK, the agreement traditionally takes the form of the government granting or recognising self-regulatory status through the award of a Royal Charter.

The Privy Council Office, not unsurprisingly, endorse the view of the National Consumer Council and state that incorporation by Royal Charter should primarily be in the public interest. This consideration is important as it often differentiates those applying for a Royal Charter from other membership organisations, such as trade bodies and trade unions, who generally act in the interests of their members. Once a body has become incorporated by Royal Charter, then it surrenders significant aspects of the control of its internal affairs to the Privy Council. Amendments to Royal Charters can thereafter only be made with the agreement of 'The Queen in Council', and amendments to the body's by-laws require the approval of the Privy Council.

Questions about professional services, consumer protection and how professionals are regulated have been commonplace for some time. The principles of professional regulation can therefore be summarised as follows:

A profession must have a governing body that sets standards of education as a condition of entry and achievement of professional status and that sets ethical standards and professional rules that are to be observed by its members. These rules are designed primarily for the benefit of the public. Professionals in breach of such rules are subject to disciplinary action and a breach may ultimately result in the loss of professional status.

Professional regulation cannot, however, be a guarantee against the failure of professional services by individual members, nor can it be a substitute for other mechanisms for redress such as the civil and criminal courts or a substitute for the management of professional staff in the workplace. Rather, it is part of the spectrum of regulatory mechanisms which, taken together, are designed to protect consumers.

What is a learned society?

Most dictionaries will tell us that a learned society is an organisation devoted to the scholarly study of a particular field or discipline. In the case of engineering we see them as bodies that create an environment where groups of academics and practitioners with a particular shared interest may come together to undertake one or more of the following activities:

- **Share good practice.** This can take many forms, including: publishing functional standards and codes of practice, publishing peer-reviewed journals, running conferences and events, designing and delivering practitioner learning opportunities such as courses and lectures, and the operation of knowledge transfer facilities, whether physical or online.

- **Promote research and development.** Many engineering institutions either directly bid for research funds to conduct research, or they operate their own research and development fund to direct discipline specific research.

- **Build capacity.** Skills gaps and shortages are created through changes arising from a variety of factors including: demographics, technology, economic cycles, and globalisation. Engineering institutions actively participate in initiatives that attempt to mitigate the worst impacts of such changes, ranging from providing careers information to schools standards can only sensibly be developed by those with sufficient knowledge and expertise in the relevant subject or discipline. Realistically, the State can only afford to maintain expertise in a limited number of areas (eg health or defence) and thereafter relies upon social enterprises such as professional institutions to take forward this work

through to providing professional development in areas of capability deficit.

→ **Develop and promote policy position statements.** Engineering institutions have in their membership many of the technical experts that the policy makers call upon when seeking to develop new policy. The institutions often publish factual statements that are not influenced by self-interest and therefore help such policy makers by presenting a balanced view.

→ **Provide peer networking opportunities.** A lot of the knowledge that is held is tacit. The opportunity to meet others with similar experiences allows such tacit knowledge to be explored and when appropriate captured for the benefit of others.

All of the above are underpinned by or contribute to the standards work that permeates the history of professional engineers that I mentioned at the beginning of this chapter. Whether you are considering individual standards of competence or collective standards of goods and services, standards can only sensibly be developed by those with sufficient knowledge and expertise in the relevant subject or discipline that is under review. Realistically, the State can only afford to maintain expertise in a limited number of areas (eg health or defence) and thereafter relies upon social enterprises such as professional institutions to take forward this work.

Conclusions

The UK engineering profession has evolved over the last 200 years to its current state of play, whereby it is able to set and regulate its own standards of professional competence and practice relevant to each of the 36 disciplines of engineering that are licensed by the Engineering Council. To achieve this, each individual member of the relevant professional institution has given a personal commitment not only to their own professional development but also to the development of others. These professionals have also agreed to be bound by a code of conduct and to behave in an ethical manner for the good of the wider society that they serve, thereby earning them the respect of that society.

A Royal College of Teaching, if supported by all stakeholders including teachers, central and local government, and the unions, could have a similar impact on the teaching profession. The College would need to be recognised as a qualifying body with a collegiate model that addressed the differing needs of each subject discipline and the ability to assess individual competence of trainee teachers, while obliging those that have already qualified to maintain their competence. As a learned society, it would also need to be recognised as a source of expertise and an essential contributor to policy and curriculum development and assessment and to approving the spectrum of teaching methods. The educational landscape is currently littered with the successes and failures of past initiatives. Perhaps now is the time for the teaching profession to request its own 'committee of inquiry' to clear the space for a new social enterprise, a Royal College of Teaching, which has the potential to provide the long-term stability in education that our children deserve.

Further voices

Gerard Kelly – Editor, Times Education Supplement

Those who doubt that teachers care about their profession should visit our website – tesconnect.com. On any given day, or more precisely evening, thousands of them will be exchanging lesson plans and professional advice that they themselves have created. These resources are downloaded at the rate of 600,000 a day. Put another way, teachers are using their own time and ingenuity in 600,000 ways daily to improve their teaching and the education of their pupils.

That teachers are doing this for themselves is a wholly good and desirable thing. It is a muscular expression of the latent power and professional pride that teachers possess. But it would be foolish to pretend that the profession has not been harmed by the absence of a body that can advise, formulate and defend best professional practice in a non-partisan way.

Transient politicians, non-teaching amateurs and opinionated newspaper columnists have filled this void, to the detriment of teachers and the confusion of pupils and parents.

It doesn't have to be this way. The profession needs a Royal College of Teaching, owned, run and directed by it. Because if teachers do not own their profession, then others with more conflicted intentions surely will.

> if teachers do not own their profession, then others with more conflicted intentions surely will

John Bangs – Honorary Visiting Fellow, Cambridge University, and former Head of Education, National Union of Teachers

The abolition of the General Teaching Council (GTC) sent all sorts of wrong messages about the future of the teaching profession in England. It looked as if the profession itself had acquiesced in taking a step backwards in defining its own status. Nothing, however, could be further from the truth. The lesson to be learnt from the GTC's fate is that imposing a professional body on teachers is doomed to fail. That is why the initiative to establish a Royal College of Teaching is very welcome. Such a body could take over the responsibility for setting teachers' professional standards. It could coordinate and publicise quality professional development such as that which is provided by teacher and subject organisations. It could provide a professional site for teachers and their organisations to come together to discuss educational developments. However, above all, it should be seen as a body which will add value to teachers' professional lives. In short it has to be seen by teachers as theirs. The debate on how establish a college has real potential. I hope it will lead to something which teachers will own and value and which will raise the status of teaching as a profession.

Sir Tim Brighouse – Non-Executive Director, RM, and former Schools Commissioner for London ; and Bob Moon – Professor of Education, Open University

Teaching is one of the most important professions in our country. Without teachers, it is arguable we would struggle to claim to be a civilised society founded on justice, liberty and freedom – never mind a place where we know our children will encounter a group of professionals committed to treating them not as they (often infuriatingly) are, but as they might become. Through their infectious enthusiasm, commitment to standards and professional skill, teachers enable our future generations not just to acquire the skills knowledge and habits to lead a fulfilled life but to think for themselves and act for others.

Yet uniquely this profession suffers from few – and haphazardly organised – opportunities for professional development and teachers are treated with mistrust by government. Their intellectual curiosity, which is the foundation of all they do, is left to chance. That's why we need a Royal College of Teaching – to speak for the profession, to resist on occasion Secretaries of State when they are tempted to cross the political–professional line, to maintain standards both of the profession and its professional development opportunities, and, in doing so, to safeguard our society's claim to be civilised.

Toni Fazeali – Chief Executive, Institute for Learning
We welcome the idea of a new Royal College of Teaching for school teachers. We know that it is important for teachers to have a membership organisation of their own, whose primary focus is on professional matters throughout their careers, in whichever schools they may work. We hope that the College will open up the wider world of research in teaching and learning for members and give new opportunities for teachers to collaborate with each other. The Institute for Learning is the independent professional body for individual teachers and trainers across further education and skills, and we look forward to working in partnership with a new college for teachers in schools.

Becky Francis – Director, Academies Commission, and Professor of Education, King's College London

There is overwhelming evidence showing that teaching quality is the key element in successful educational outcomes, and this illustrates the importance of professional development and evidence-informed practice. As the Academies Commission highlighted, school autonomy and innovation needs to be supported by teacher development and a culture of peer learning, in order to get the best from an autonomous system. An independent Royal College of Teaching is urgently needed to build such a culture, to enhance the quality and professional status of teaching, and to disseminate best practice. One of the College's key objectives should be the encouragement of school-to-school collaboration, including peer challenge and support.

Teaching as a profession is unique. It is made up of experts in every subject imaginable who are simultaneously expert in the science of pedagogy and skilled in the art of teaching. Teachers can be found in formal and non-formal settings in schools, colleges, universities, hospitals, businesses, factories, homes, military establishments and youth groups. In no other profession do the practitioners come from such a wide variety of backgrounds or practise in such a wide variety of settings with such a wide variety of qualifications and training.

And yet, unlike other professions, teaching has no single body which independently represents, pulls together and supports the development of the myriad professionals and organisations that work to support them. Such a body is vital for the long-term growth, health and independence of a profession.

The College could play a critical role in defending the long-term development of the profession and the career-long development of everyone who calls themselves a teacher, while informing and advising governments on shorter-term political goals.

Steve Munby – Chief Executive, CfBT Education Trust

As someone who is passionate about school leadership and the difference that effective leaders can make, I am very keen to endorse the concept of a Royal College of Teaching. We know from the excellent work of people like Professor Viviane Robinson (*Student-Centred Leadership*, 2011), that leaders are at their most powerful and influential when participating in, and leading, teacher learning and development. A Royal College of Teaching, led by education professionals, focusing on evidence-based research and the professional development of teachers, would be a great step-forward for education in this country. It would help to give greater status to the teaching profession and attract more of our talented young people to want to have a career in teaching. It would need to be led by credible education professionals and to build its credibility through direct engagement with the teaching profession.

Over the last two decades, the need to improve both standards and equity
in education in England has spurred the government to action. While some
initiatives have relied on the professionalism of teachers, many have tended
towards direction from the centre. Casting teachers as 'delivery agents'
ultimately undermines achieving the level of professionalism present in the
teaching forces of the highest performing jurisdictions. I believe we should
learn from the other key professions. A Royal College of Teaching provides
an institutional focus for the processes, which we need. Professional self-
regulation is vital – not unproblematic in its implementation in various
settings over time but potent in maintaining and enhancing practice in
areas such as medicine. 'Trust teachers' has become a mantra in some
quarters. However, this remains empty rhetoric unless specific mechanisms
are put in place to develop and sustain the processes needed to form a
profession which enjoys systemic, evidence-based enhancement and wide
public trust. We need to move away from the unclear lines of responsibility
which have pervaded teacher–government relations during phases
of intensive, centrally led school-improvement strategies. Instead, an
educational analogue of a medical royal college shifts the locus of control
to the profession but with mechanisms for self-regulated development and
enhancement of teaching standards.

John Roberts – Chief Executive, Edapt

Edapt advocates a Royal College of Teaching and recognises the potential
it has to raise the status of the teaching profession and allow teachers
to reclaim their schools and classrooms from political interference. The
ongoing development of skills is fundamental to driving a self-improving,
respected and autonomous profession. It is well recognised that attracting
and retaining teachers of the highest quality is the driver for the very best
educational standards for our young people. A Royal College of Teaching,
independent from government, should enthuse both schools and teachers
to promote teacher development, specialism and career progression. In
order to promote professional autonomy we also understand the need

for a highly respected, trusted and impartial body to represent teachers on pedagogical issues based upon evidence and research. An academic and apolitical Royal College of Teaching would be very well positioned to provide such representation. Edapt holds the promotion of professional development as one of its core values and would extend its development fund to enable teachers to access such opportunities provided by a Royal College of Teaching. We look forward to supporting its development.

Chris Pope – Chair of the PTI-led Commission to explore the establishment of a new member-driven College of Teaching, and Co-Director, Prince's Teaching Institute

It is my privilege to work every year with hundreds of highly motivated and dedicated teachers, who lead and participate in the activities of The Prince's Teaching Institute (PTI). So it is perhaps not surprising that when we have mentioned the idea of a new member-driven Royal College of Teaching at PTI events, they have shown considerable enthusiasm for the idea of a universally respected body that would celebrate and uphold professional standards. Clearly, there is much devil in the detail of just what this new entity would do and how it would do it, and this defining process, as well as achieving buy-in from the profession, will take time. But, to quote a PTI event participant, 'the fact that it will take a long time is not an excuse not to do it, but it is a reason to start now'.

the fact
that it will
take a long time
is not an excuse not to do it,
but it is a reason to start now